Foundational Techniques for Mastering Environment and Character Concept Art

This is a comprehensive guide to the process of generating ideas for creating character and environment art. The book shows comprehensive workshops and techniques to embed the fundamentals of designing characters and environments for games and film. The underlying process is explained and demonstrated to give a straightforward approach that anyone can use. Using these processes, you will be able to produce designs that are straight out of your imagination.

This book teaches you how to use your imagination to design characters and environments. As well as evolving these ideas through the various stages of ideation, the book covers both environment and character workflows. The book is accompanied by a series of videos breaking down the process of research and creation, as well as additional exercises and breakdowns of good workflow for readers to follow along with as they develop their skills.

This book will be of great interest to anyone looking to gain a grounding in the theory and practice of concept art for character and environments. It will be particularly useful for students on Game Art courses.

Lee Stocks is a Senior Lecturer and Course Leader for Game Art courses at Leeds Beckett University, United Kingdom. Lee's practice and research is centred around Games Design and Games Art, and is heavily influenced by communication and storytelling. His body of work and teaching practices range from game and level design to concept art.

Lee has made contributions to the creative sector since 2001, working as a game designer and concept artist/illustrator. The projects he has worked on range from online games, through to film/television and illustration. The fundamentals of art and design are at the core of what he teaches. Observation and drawing/digital painting being the two areas that he has identified as a catalyst for improving imagination and creativity.

Game design theory is one of the key areas that has benefited from this approach in his teaching. Lee has identified how idea generation and iteration are key factors in enhancing student's development. So, implementing the teaching of these observation and drawing/digital painting processes has become his primary technique.

Foundational Techniques for Mastering Environment and Character Concept Art

Lee Stocks

CRC Press
Taylor & Francis Group
Boca Raton London New York

CRC Press is an imprint of the
Taylor & Francis Group, an **informa** business

Designed cover image: Lee Stocks

First edition published 2026
by CRC Press

2385 NW Executive Center Drive, Suite 320, Boca Raton FL 33431

and by CRC Press

4 Park Square, Milton Park, Abingdon, Oxon, OX14 4RN

CRC Press is an imprint of Taylor & Francis Group, LLC

ISBN: 9781032814704 (hbk)
ISBN: 9781032769899 (pbk)
ISBN: 9781003500032 (ebk)
ISBN: 9781032814711 (eBook+)

DOI: 10.1201/9781003500032

Typeset in Sabon
by KnowledgeWorks Global Ltd.
Access the Instructor Resources/Support Material: www.routledge.com/9781032769899

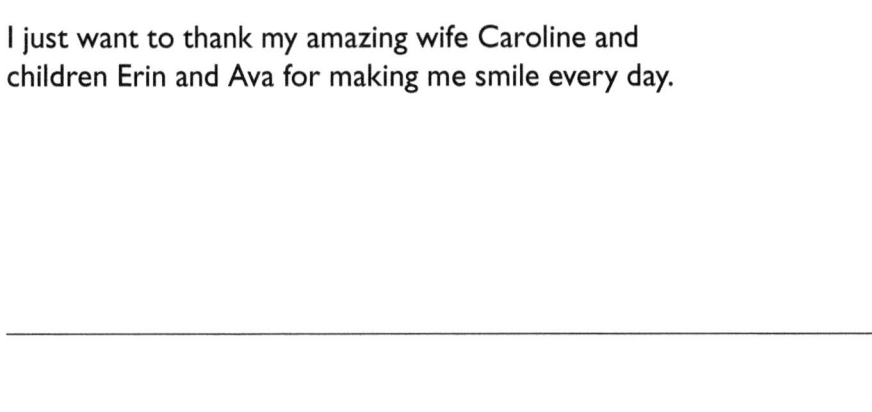

I just want to thank my amazing wife Caroline and children Erin and Ava for making me smile every day.

Contents

Foreword

by Andrew Sandham

For a visual creative, mastery of concept and environment art is like being handed the keys to the toyshop. And believe me, you don't need to tell me how important these art forms are—I've been there.

Cutting my teeth in the wild west days of the games industry at Bullfrog Productions in the early '90s, I started as a junior artist, concepting characters for Magic Carpet and other early titles. Even back then, it was clear that the concept artist was the foundational pillar for how a game would look and feel.

Alas, with my penchant for drawing musclebound superhero types, one of my first lessons in character concepting came quickly. To paraphrase the classic design principle: in this case, "form follows fiction". No one—least of all the players—expects to see a 260 lb. space marine soaring gracefully across the desert on a Magic Carpet.

Aptly named, Magic Carpet became a metaphor for my nascent journey into game development—climbing aboard and never looking back, later joining Core Design to work on the original Tomb Raider series, where the toyshop doors were once more flung open, as I was tasked with concepting, designing and building entire level environments from the ground up. It didn't take long (perhaps a little too long, judging by early player feedback) to realise that strong, clear previsualisation is key to effective level and environment design. Without it, core visual and design ideas quickly become muddied in translation—especially now, within the multi-team pipelines that define modern game and film production.

Not just through my own missteps, but by witnessing others, I've seen the other side of the process too. Weak or inexperienced concept work can cause production bottlenecks, miscommunication across teams and dreaded feature creep. Understanding scope, pipeline and how to clearly communicate ideas is vital—and that's where Lee's expertise comes to the fore.

Having worked with Lee for several years, I've seen him not only produce robust, compelling concept and environment designs for both personal and commercial projects, but also mentor students to do the same. Through his Game Art course, he's helped shape countless emerging artists into industry-ready professionals—creatives who understand the clarity and consistency required to hand over their work to art and design departments as functioning blueprints, rather than becoming spanners in the works. And now, Lee is handing that knowledge over to you.

The book you're holding isn't just a how-to—it's a roadmap built on years of commercial industry practice. It lays out the foundational techniques and processes needed to deliver clear, purposeful and inspiring character concept and environment art for both games and film.

These pages will help you forge your own key to the toyshop. And when you're finally holding it, open the door, climb aboard the Magic Carpet—and maybe, this time, leave the space marine behind.

Andy Sandham, MSc, FHEA Game & Digital Design
Specialist, Academic, Educator and Author of *Teaching Video
Game Design Fundamentals* Sheffield, June 2025

Introduction

Thank you for buying this book. All the lessons contained within are tried and tested ways in which to develop your skills as a concept artist. All of the tasks and examples are hard earned from personal experience from my career as a concept artist illustrator as well as from working in higher education over the past 20 years (depending on when you read this book). The technical skills that are required to work as a concept artist are just a part of the process. Underneath, this is also how you generate ideas through research and iterate upon them. As well as the personal attributes like determinations and failure, which are key to an artist's development. All of these skills combine together to form who we are as an artist. Over the course of this book, we will explore them in depth, along with other skills that will help your work and process.

This book contains examples of work and detailed breakdowns of the key fundamental skills that are required to work in this particular field. These key skills will be developed through the tasks and demos contained on its pages. These tasks are designed to be repeated and will embed the principles needed for your journey as a concept artist.

The journey you are now on will be full of highs and lows but with dedication and a positive attitude the skills you will learn will be lifechanging.

This book is aimed at people wanting to start that process of developing their skills as a concept artist, at a beginner level or entry level concept artist role. This book will show you how to generate ideas, research, sketch and block out ideas and iterate upon them.

Both the hard and soft skills that you will learn can be applied across a wide range of creative areas and not just screen media like games and film.

This book will not go into depth regarding how to detail and render, but we will touch upon this as we move through the book. There are many other books and resources available in the market that cover how to detail and produce a finished product in much greater detail, and these will be named at the end of the book.

WHAT WILL BE COVERED IN THIS BOOK

This book will cover the starting principles of how to start your journey as a concept artist. The two main areas that will be explored are that of environment concept art and character concept art. I will not be delving into creature design but a lot of the principles covered in character design are directly applicable to this particular area.

We will look at the discipline of concept art and how it pertains to environment and character. We will explore research and how we build a visual library. We will look at storytelling and how to embed this into your work and practice. We will also look at how to interpret a brief and soft skills that you will need to successfully interpret it. And finally this book will cover the main fundamentals that underpin each discipline.

This book will cover the techniques and exercises to strengthen the main fundamentals that underpin each discipline.

The tasks in this book are designed to be repeated with different reference or subject matter. You should be looking to pick and choose which tasks work best for your current skill level and are resonating with you. Also, because this book is a mixture of environment and character concept art processes, you should be focusing on the tasks that you are interested in developing skills for.

This book will show how to use basic 3D in Blender to build environment scenes and create rough block outs, which can then be used as a guide when painting or drawing. The 3D techniques I will be showing are very easy to pick up. These techniques won't delve into modelling or editing meshes but are purely concerned with composition, aiding perspective and used to solve complex staging problems.

Finally, this book will show you the tasks you should be doing to get your skills up to a good level in the areas of character and environment design. The exercises in this book are the fastest ways that I have found to get a beginner's skills up to where they need to be, to start creating meaningful works.

ADDITIONAL LEARNING RESOURCES

To enhance your learning experience, this book is accompanied by exclusive video content demonstrating the drawing and painting exercises covered in some chapters. These videos offer step-by-step guidance, visual techniques and practical tips to help you develop your skills more confidently and intuitively within the field of concept art. Whether you're a beginner or looking to refine your artistic approach further, the video demonstrations provide clear, hands-on approaches to the written material, bringing the creative process to life. These can be downloaded from the book's webpage at: www.routledge.com/9781032769899

THINGS THAT WON'T BE COVERED IN THIS BOOK

This is not a book showing you how to render or detail work to a finished level. This book covers the 90% that happens before the rendering or detail phases. (Rendering and finished detail is a little bit like the cherry and sprinkles on top of the ice cream. Its flashy and adds flavour but the thing that holds everything together is the ice cream and cone.) It is easy to see why these finished details are appealing as a new artist but it's important to concentrate on the fundamentals, shape design and getting the read of the work correct.

Another area that won't be covered in detail is colour. Colour is such a vast subject area and there are many other books and online tutorials that cover this area of art and design, that we won't be exploring. Not addressing colour in this book will in no way impact what we are hoping to achieve in this book. Value is the main way we will be communicating, and this is the most efficient way to work as a beginner.

This book will not cover photobashing techniques. (Photobashing is the technique of using pictures in a painting through overlaying, blending and positioning. The reason for not covering these techniques is because of how advanced they are and how problematic they can be for people who don't understand the fundamentals of visual communication. The technique of photobashing can be a fast way of establishing detail and texture in a digital image. However, people who don't have a firm grasp of the fundamentals tend to end up with really flat and uncanny looking images when using these techniques. There is a place for these techniques in the production of concept art but not at this level.

Chapter 1

Personal attributes

INTRODUCTION TO PERSONAL ATTRIBUTES

Personal attributes are an incredibly important topic when we are talking about becoming a concept artist, but probably not in the way you think. There are of course the personal attributes that refer to the technical aspects of creating works. These are things like understanding the fundamentals of drawing/painting, techniques, traditional and in software like Photoshop, as well as a good understanding of design principles and how to communicate visually. However, there are also a number of other personal attributes that are desirable when producing works, and in the end getting a job as a concept artist.

For simplicity, I am going to split these personal attributes into two categories to differentiate them.

PERSONAL ATTRIBUTES WHILE PAINTING AND DRAWING

When you are starting to create works, it's easy to think it's just about finding inspiration, grabbing reference and then painting or drawing a beautiful environment or character. Sadly, it's never that easy. There are a number of things that happen and influence how successful a piece is. And this takes the form of your character attributes. These are the things that underpin how and why you work in a certain way.

When you are right at the start of a project, you need to be able to generate ideas, and I will go through some practical things you can do to enhance this, later in the book. But attitude has the single biggest impact on how you work and the quality of your work. When looking for ideas, it's important that you explore as many different things as possible. It's also really important to try and find solutions or options. It's very common to stumble across what seems like a great idea only, for it becomes an average as you work through it. This is why not settling for your first good idea and continuing to explore the topic

DOI: 10.1201/9781003500032-1

is vital. Perseverance is key in this early stage of research and idea generation. It can be difficult to maintain striving to find unique ideas, but I would encourage anyone in this early design phase to be curious and look outside of your comfort zone for new and unique ideas.

PERSONAL ATTRIBUTES OTHER

As a concept artist, you are expected to generate solutions or options and deliver these as paintings or drawings that communicate their purpose and story for the intellectual property (IP) you are developing. To do this, a concept artist must have personal characteristics to help this happen. Most of these soft skills are the difference between good work and exceptional work. These can often make the difference in how long your career lasts also.

The soft skills and personal attributes that I am talking about are things like determination, and an ability to get on with people. I can't emphasise this enough for beginner artists and designers, it's so important. We work on this a lot on the courses I teach on. It's not just what you make, it's how you present it, in every sense. Always try to be humble and non-negative when talking about your work and that of others. A person who has empathy towards others and brings a positive outlook is a very desirable trait to have.

DETERMINATION

Determination can come in lots of different flavours, in terms of how it manifests itself in people. There is the quiet just getting on with it type of person, or the visually active, exuberant person. Both are fine as long as this doesn't impact the people you are working and interacting with. The main reason determination is an essential soft skill is because of the nature of the work you are undertaking as a concept artist. The role requires you to generate lots of ideas, continuously and trying to define an idea that doesn't exist yet. This leads to lots of back and forth feedback on your designs. Determination is an essential factor in being successful in this area. As a designer, you have to be able to pivot your designs and generate new ideas in a relatively short amount of time, based on sometimes vague feedback. Never take feedback personally (easier said than done sometimes), everyone is striving for the best designs and they are often only found after lots of hours of toil.

It's often beneficial to take some time to let the feedback settle before starting on new designs. This really helps in assessing where the client or director is wanting the direction designs to go. I have dived straight back into new designs based on feedback in the past and missed the direction at times. Letting it settle is a great way of avoiding this.

EMPATHY

Empathy is my favourite soft skill that I like to talk to students about before they start their journey into concept art and depending on how you look at it. It's also a massive part of your design process. Although some people might disagree with me on that one. Empathy is a massive part of the design process of a concept artist. Concept artists, as I have talked about previously need to be able to get into the head of both the client and the characters/environments that you are designing. With that in mind, it's really important that you can interpret what is needed for the things you are designing and building. What does the brief require you to do, and what does the art director or client want to see in your designs? This requires a degree of empathy, being able to put yourself in their shoes and look at the project holistically from a zoomed-out perspective. This is often quite hard to do, people are complicated, and projects are multifaceted. Trying to understand the larger view can often be facilitated through listening more and asking broader questions than just what's my canvas size?

The other important area that requires empathy is in the designing of characters and environments themselves. The worlds and people that you are building should feel real and the only way to do this convincingly is through design empathy. As a concept artist you are expected to create beautiful things that are interesting to the viewer or player. The visuals you create need to be underpinned with history and story. Before we commit to drawing/painting anything, we need to understand what the space is that we are designing and who the character(s) is. This is where empathy comes in and it plays a crucial role in the design process.

For environments, we need to understand what the rules of the world are, what type of climate it has and who lives within it. So, we can ask ourselves what shapes the space? Once we have a grip on the broad detail of the world, we can start asking it questions, like who lives here and what do they do? We slowly work through this until we have rules for our environment.

When designing characters, I find it useful to ask myself environment questions first like the ones above. The reason for this is because we are all reflective of the environment we live in and to get a grip of your characters, you first have to understand the world they occupy.

Once you have this environment overview, you can then safely move onto the details of your character. Who are they and what do they want? What drives them and what could they look like based on this information?

Of course, the more time you spend defining the environments and character, the more options you will have for your designs. This in my opinion is the secret to good designs and putting yourself in the shoes of the spaces you are designing and the characters you are creating is a great way to work.

Chapter 2

Concept art overview

INTRODUCTION

Concept art is the imagining and designing of worlds and the things contained within them. This discipline is usually associated with games, film and television. The main job of a concept artist is to generate ideas and guide the style of a production, whatever that might be.

There are many routes into the role of concept artist and no set path. A foundational understanding of art in general is in my opinion essential. Good drawing and communication skills are also essential. These skills are what we will be developing and focusing on throughout this book and what we will develop through the tasks.

Concept artists typically fit into one of two very general roles within this discipline, either a generalist or a specialist. This of course depends on a number of factors, including size of company you are working for, or the length of the project you are working on. So please take this over simplified definition with a pinch of salt.

CONCEPT DESIGN V CONCEPT ART

A concept artist and a concept designer, depending on who you talk to are two slightly different disciplines, with a significant amount of overlap. I prefer to think of these jobs as different with the outputs being different enough to merit this distinction. It is worth noting that it is the same fundamental skills and visual design approaches that underpin both these disciplines.

Concept artists tend to come up with overarching ideas and rough ideas, suggestions for the mood and tone of the project and the things within it. Concept designers, still design and come up with ideas, but are far more proficient in producing nailed down "finished" ideas that would appear and work in the intellectual property (IP) you are designing for.

You also tend to see concept artists working across games, film and TV. Whereas concept designers are far more prevalent in film and TV. This is down to the physical objects that have to be created for the live action

DOI: 10.1201/9781003500032-2

medium, in conjunction to the 3D digital assets and props that are designed and built for games.

GENERALIST

A generalist is a term used to describe concept artists who are proficient in a number of different areas and able to produce a variety of work, such as character and vehicle design. A generalist would also be able to produce work for a number of different genres, such as, fantasy, science, fiction or gothic.

A generalist will use most of the same tools as a specialist and work broadly in the same way but typically won't be someone who will produce really high-end art works in one particular area. There are some exceptions of course, but generally speaking, these types of artists main aim is to produce ideas and to visualise them quickly.

The nature of being a generalist means they work across such a wide area, they aren't going to produce super high-end works in a given area. The standard will still be at a high level and professionally presented but there will be concessions due to the multi-disciplinary nature of the work produced.

There is a good amount of work out there for generalists, with a consistent quality portfolio. Most generalists working will have a strong grasp on the fundamentals in their area and have a strong portfolio of diverse works. Because of this there is work out there for these types of artists.

SPECIALIST

A specialist is a type of concept artist who focuses in one, or occasionally a couple of key disciplines. This could be for instance, only focusing on environment art. These types of artists would produce exceptional designs, due to the amount of time they have under their belts working in that particular discipline. The high quality of their work means these artists have no problem finding work in their discipline. These people have a track record and work that shows specialist knowledge in the things they produce. I would class artists like Jaime Jones and Ian McQue all in this. Both of these artists have a clear visual style, exceptional body of work within the specialism they work in. This has been epic environments in the case of Jaime Jones and vehicle and environment design for Ian McQue.

These types of artists are the focal point for the design process within their individual disciplines and are the people who have the power through their artwork, to really shape and impact the projects that they work on. This is through the work they create and through the visual style.

We should however take these broad distinctions with a pinch of salt. There are of course going to be exceptions and exceptional individuals to the rule.

Chapter 3

Visual library

INTRODUCTION TO VISUAL LIBRARY

Your visual library is in essence, the way your brain uses image reference that you have stored in your head. This can be anything from, you walking down the street on y our way to the shops, when you were in class at school or an advert in a magazine you saw while having a coffee. All of the things that you absorb from the world around you. The human brain is trained to observe and then discard anything that it deems unnecessary or unimportant. The unnecessary or unimportant is a subjective thing depending on the person observing.

Your visual library is hugely important for concept artists. This is where all of your ideas come from and because the job of a concept artists is all about ideas, it's easy to see why this is so important.

We can't store all our ideas in our heads, and this is where our digital visual library comes in. When looking online or on social media I often stumble across photographs or artwork that inspires me. I then save these images online on Pinterest. Anything that you find visually inspiring you should try and store online on Pinterest or other reference sites. That way we can access this whenever we need it.

Artists should always be adding to an online visual reference library and saving ideas.

Your visual library is the visual information that you have retained from the world around you, from your life. To clarify, this can cover lots of different areas and level of detail. These pictorial memories carry more than just raw details about what the space looked like. It also carries the details of what it felt like to be there. This might sound incidental but imagine someone showing you a picture of a raging waterfall and then comparing it to actually being stood next to it. A good visual library is essential to your success as a concept artist.

Here are the two different types of visual references you would find in an artist's visual library:

- You might remember a childhood beach holiday, where you made sand-castles. This memory might be fragmented and feel more like snippets from the past.

DOI: 10.1201/9781003500032-3

- This could also be the reference you have gathered on Pinterest or any other site that allows you to save visual reference.

Both these types of visual references offer benefits to a concept artist. The first one, or the lived memory as we will call it has lots of flavours and feelings associated with it, but it is just that, a memory. It lacks form and doesn't exist visually. Even if you have taken a picture of the moment, it won't feel the same as the event itself.

Take the picture below…

Photograph of a pumpkin field.

I am the only person who would look at this picture and see the memory of the experience.

This is a photo I took of a pumpkin field that I took just before Halloween while out with my family. I remember the morning we spent their very well and all the associated feeling that went along with it. But to look at the image it doesn't contain all that information. The camera and photo is unbiased and the context of the photo is within the person looking at it. I will always have the memories associated with the photo but if I was trying to design an artwork around the themes of say Halloween, I would need more visual reference in the form of pictures and images gathered, on say Pinterest to make that happen and have the flavour that I wanted to come across.

This leads to one of the fundamental strategies that can lead to better work. Use lots of visual references to inspire and underpin your work.

RESEARCH

Research is the process of gathering visual reference to inspire and guide the work you create. As you can imagine is a very important and often lengthy task that happens on all projects. Research is without question the most important process you will do as a concept artist. Research is responsible for the ideas you generate and the tone of which these ideas are represented in your work.

Research is the work you do before and during a project to generate ideas and evolve them into images or assets.

Research falls into two categories, **Visual** and **Non-visual**. Visual research is usually in the form of moodboards. Moodboards are a collection of images found on the internet and collaged together in a document or online, then used to help the creation process.

Snowy moodboard.

This snow moodboard, for example, would be useful for establishing the space and compositions of the world you are intending to build, if we were building a world covered in snow.

Research is fundamental in generating and iterating ideas.

Research can be split up into lots of sub areas when working on a project and we will go through them below:

- **Non-visual Research**
- **Visual Research**

- Initial Response Research
- Tonal Research
- Practical Research

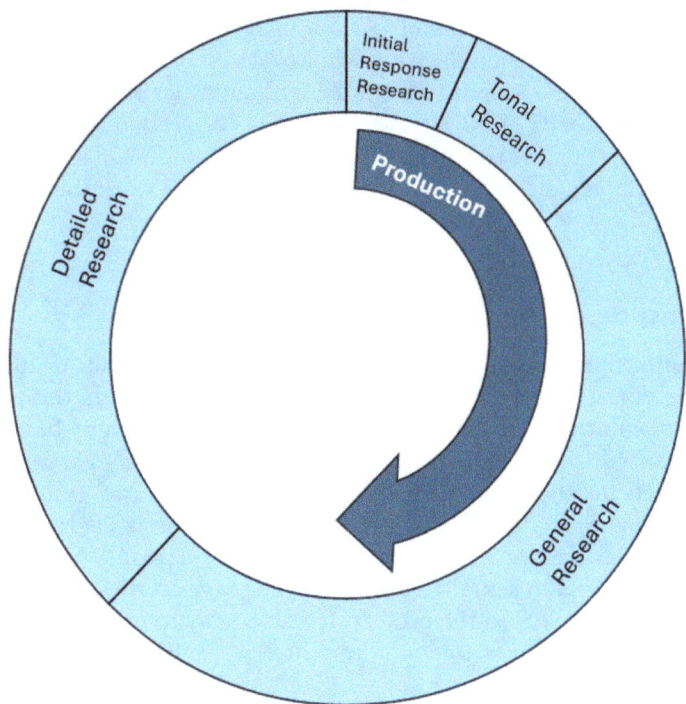

Chart of workflow on a project.

Non-visual research

Non-visual research is an often the forgotten part of visual design. As artists, we are always focused on what the things we are trying to make looks like. At the start of any project, I would strongly advise reading and trying to understand the subject area you are designing for. Essentially, this is the context in which the work you will create sits. Now this is massive for a designer. Not understanding the themes and subject area you are designing for can lead to work that fails to hit its mark and fail to communicate what you are aiming for in your designs.

At the start of any project, I have found that reading around the subject area in the early stages of the research phase is the best way to supercharge your research before you start looking at visual reference.

I also try and watch documentaries around the subject area during this early phase of development to give me a deeper understanding of what the subject area is. The watching of films and documentaries either at the start of a project or during the early part of a project can really help you get emersed in the world you are trying to create.

There are a few caveats to this that you should be made aware of while using this technique. You have to be careful to let the things you are watching enhance your work, inform and not to dominate it. This means not taking the things you are watching and hearing wholesale.

Sometimes on a live project you may be sent out a fact pack of information. This should be looked at during the early phase of production, to help your work stay relevant to the thing you are trying to produce. However, this is meant as a jumping off point for concept artists and the work they are aiming to produce.

Initial response research

Initial response research is the first idea that pops into your head and the first thing you gather and search for on a given project. If the project is a rundown cabin in the woods, your initial thoughts might be the cabin from a film Evil Dead 2 or an old shed in your neighbour's garden. So, you would search for these images in Google or Pinterest and grab images of the cabin from Evil Dead 2 and pictures of overgrown sheds. You might then find similar images or make other mental connections that take you to other areas of visual research. You would then save all these before further defining your approach to the project. It's also okay to let the mind wander at this stage of the process to try to find interesting "ins" to the project you are working on.

There are a couple of pointers I would suggest at this stage of researching. The first one is, build a couple of moodboards fairly quick of your initial responses to the brief you are working on. What happens with a lot of the students I teach is they tend to grab lots of other artists work. You need to quickly move away from this. I think it's fine to have a couple of mood-boards of inspirational reference as something to aim at. However, grabbing too much of this as reference can lead to getting stuck and producing copies of this work, which isn't good. I would say once you have a moodboard or two, leave it behind and then switch to building a tonal moodboard or practical moodboards to start the idea generation process.

This is your initial response research.

TONAL RESEARCH

Tonal research is how tonally and emotionally you want the project to feel to the viewer. For example, if you have dark moody sci-fi images, you would expect the project to have a dark sci-fi feel to the work you create.

These tonal moodboards will have images on them that you might use for inspiration in terms of the things you design, but the reality is that most of these images will be there to scope the tone rather than hard details.

Tonal moodboards are often used as a centre point in the design process. And usually when working on larger projects, represent the aim or outcome of the project as a whole. Tonal moodboards are often used as key areas of reference for a design team. One good tonal moodboard containing 6–8 images can keep an entire design team on track. If we consider the tonal moodboards as the emotions, we want the player or viewer to feel as they look at your environments or characters, it's easy to see how important they are from a production perspective. These types of moodboards are often hardest to build and this is understandable given how complex human emotions are. It's also extremely difficult to convey complex emotions in a visual way. I mean think about it, how can you convey regret in 6–8 images? However, it's worth mastering this art, not just for your own process but also for the benefits it brings when working as a design team.

Often tonal moodboards tend to get overlooked or bundled into other visual reference moodboards. This is a bit of a mistake if you are starting out, and it's worth making sure you produce one of these for each project, to keep the project on track and of the correct tone.

Also, when dealing with emotions, try to think about them in ranges or describe with a connection word for specificity. For example, how regretful is the character you are designing? A 1 or a 10 on an imaginary scale? Or anything in between? Is it deep regret or regret tinged with anger? All these nuances make a difference to the way you approach the design process. Things are rarely black or white when it comes to human emotions or feelings. And to be super clear, emotions also apply to environments. You can have an angry forest or a regretful river.

DETAILED RESEARCH

Detailed research is the final, if you like, stage of research. Detailed research happens once you have a core idea (based on lots of visual references and painstaking thinking around the design you want), have iterated upon these ideas and are now focussed on detailing.

Detailing is the act of describing visually your ideas. Detail moodboards are usually themed around the objects or things you want to describe on either an environment or a character. For instance, for a detailed character moodboard you would have separate moodboards for hair, equipment, clothing, etc. The reason for this is to accurately represent the objects associated with the character. This is also a great way to add important story details to the character you are designing. If your character is designed really well, then these detail elements act as flavouring for the audience or viewers. Everything on the characters you create is an opportunity for storytelling.

Detailed environment moodboards will contain buildings, objects and other street furniture contained within the scene. Again, you would have separate moodboards for each element, so when you are painting or drawing you can generate more interesting design ideas. And like with characters, everything you put in the environment is a chance for storytelling. With environments, it's really important that you consider where these objects are placed.

Detailed research should be the easiest type of research to do. The reason for this is because you should have a good idea of what you are producing, as well as the tone and things you want to achieve from the design. One important thing to remember when grabbing detailed reference is what drew you to the reference in the first place. If I choose a character design that I found during my research and choose to add it to a moodboard, what parts of that character are inspiring me. And this can be anything, it could be the backpack the character is carrying, the shoes they are wearing or just the shapes of the clothes they are wearing. Knowing this will really help when it comes to painting/drawing and help you avoid using the image you have gathered in its entirety. I often see students who see an image of an amazing character design or beautiful environment and just recreate it. I get it, but it offers very little working like this. This character or environment already exists. A healthier way to work is by naming what you like about the images you pick. This usually leads to elements of an image being used and a far better end product.

RESOURCES

People starting out down their art journey today for the first time are really lucky to have the wealth of resources that are available today. There are so many different ways of finding the information and inspiration to get the creative juices flowing. Below is a breakdown of what resources are available and how I would use them for projects and teaching.

When I first started out on my creative journey and career, there wasn't the internet or drawing tablets to design and build works. My main source of information and inspiration was in the local library, things I found in magazines and most importantly the world around me. I kind of miss those days, you never really found the perfect book or image but everything that you did find you pawed over and really analysed.

Today's creative however, has the world at their fingertips. Search engines can conjure up any image or piece of information your imagination can think of. This can cause a bit of visual and information overload for people starting out. The sheer volume of what you can look at is scary. Don't worry however, these are good problems to have.

With so many resources available I am going to talk about the main ones that I use.

VIDEO

When talking about video I am mainly referring to videos that are available online. There are two main sites that have a high amount of content to help with the process of making art. The first place as you might have guessed is Youtube. There are so many good artists that put their work in a video format onto Youtube which is easily accessible and digestible. I have included some of these choice links at the end of the book. There is everything you could hope for to get you started here and all it requires is good use of search terms to find the videos that are useful.

The second place for good video content is Twitch. Similar to Youtube, Twitch is a live streaming service with some good, archived artist works. But where Twitch really comes into its own is on its live content. You can see many artists creating artworks live and talking through their process, which for beginner artists is priceless.

The last place for video content is Gumroad. I have used this a lot in the past but most of the really good stuff on there is behind a pay wall. In my opinion, if you find an artist whose work and process you like it might be worth seeing if they have any work on Gumroad (or a comparable site) to buy. However, this will be later down the line in terms of your development and when you have a good understanding of the work you want to create. It's also worth checking out what reviews and star ratings this type of content has. This can be a really good indicator as to what you are getting and if it's appropriate for your level and what you want to learn.

SEARCH TERMS

Search terms refers to the words you type into a search engine to find the information or images you are looking for. This is rapidly becoming more important as a designer. What you type in directly affects what results you get back. This can be an early stumbling block for designers/artists, just because the things you are looking for may not be visible because of the way you are searching for them. This all sounds obvious but in teaching for the last decade, plus I have noticed that this is an area where people can improve. I see people all the time using generic search terms like, "castles" instead of "dark snowy ruined castle by the sea", get really specific and then change these terms up as you get a handle on what images you are getting back. I would also try and use these search terms across multiple websites and apps. So, try typing these search terms into, Artstation, Youtube, Google, etc.

It's also worth exploring a few rabbit holes as you widen your searches. Often you will see multiple images that are appealing to you as a designer, in some way. It's worth making sure you are opening up new browser windows to explore them, while at the same time keeping the jumping off point in the background so you can come back to it when you have finished exploring each particular rabbit hole. It's also worth taking regular breaks when ideas are on the wane. This is a natural part of the design process and don't try to force results if they just aren't coming. Take a step back and give your mind chance to rest before you start the search again.

It is also a good idea to keep in mind why you are searching for these images and inspiration in the first place. Make sure you keep thinking about the brief you are trying to fulfil and how you want to fulfil it. It is really easy to get lost down a rabbit hole and finally emerge having completely missed the point of what you were searching for in the first place.

Chapter 4

The design brief

INTERPRETING A DESIGN BRIEF

It is impossible to discuss concept art and design in general without discussing "The Brief". The brief refers to the objectives and aims of what you are trying to achieve in the works you create. In most cases, when working in the creative sector you will be given a brief, by either the client or the art director overseeing the project. The brief that you receive can range wildly from one project to the next. Some project briefs are very specific with little room to move, and these will require you to work within quite tight constraints. Other briefs can be very vague and might require further conversations with the person leading the project for clarification. However, all the briefs you receive as a concept artist are about creating a visual design or artifact for a new or existing project.

THE SPECIFIC BRIEF

A specific brief can range from having very little freedom, to having some wiggle room when it comes to creativity and what direction you can take the project. Specific briefs often have clear deliverables, both in terms of indicative amounts of work and final outputs. There will also be clear tonal design principles that you will have to adhere to, if you want to produce appropriate work for the client or art director.

Some designers struggle with a lack of freedom but with a strict specific brief because of the perceived lack of freedom in terms of the type of work you are producing. Constraints as a designer are, in my opinion a really good thing. Having tight parameters is a really good way of eliminating white noise when it comes to researching and initial designs.

The trick with this type of brief is to enjoy the constraints and look for interesting ways into interpreting the brief. This can often be done through researching into the subject area and really focusing on who is going to be engaging with the things you produce.

DOI: 10.1201/9781003500032-4

THE IN-BETWEEN BRIEF

The in-between brief is exactly that, it sits somewhere in-between "specific" and "open" in terms of how many constraints you have to consider for your work. Broadly speaking, most briefs fall into this category. Within this brief, it's common to have wiggle room in terms of the ideas that you have been asked to generate. This process is usually a much more collaborative process that what you would typically find in a specific brief. This usually entails more constructive feedback and back and forth, with your suggestions carrying more weight. That doesn't mean however that if the client asks for an environment piece featuring an abandoned galleon grounded in the sand, that you can just build a ruined castle in the snow. But it does mean there is more scope for pushing design ideas to the edge of what would be acceptable. This is a balancing act and it's good to make detailed notes and ask lots of questions in those early meetings with the clients.

The reason for this is the person commissioning the work either doesn't have the expertise to design and build the things they need or they don't know how to approach this. But in both cases, they require your creativity in approaching the task. So, there will be some give and take when it comes to the ideas you generate.

THE OPEN BRIEF

An open brief is both a blessing and a curse, depending on your mindset as a designer. An open brief is often seen as a dream brief for new designers. An open brief usually had a clear end product in mind in terms of what you should be producing. For example, a character, of a certain time period or style, but is lacking specifics in terms of tone or how far the design is able to be pushed. The brief may also be lacking narrative cues to guide your design. Simply this just means as a designer you are having to search too wide an area, from a design point of view. One way to mitigate this is to look at the company's style and tone within the work they have produced in the past, this is usually a good indicator of the ballpark you should be aiming at.

Personally, I'm not a fan of very open briefs, I enjoy working within tighter constraints that push your ability to solve problems. If you are presented with an open brief, try to find your own constraints to help scope your ideas.

Chapter 5

Drawing and painting

INTRODUCTION TO DIGITAL PAINTING/DRAWING

Digital painting/drawing is essentially the same as traditional painting and drawing, just using digital software instead. The software I will be using throughout
the tasks and demonstrations is Photoshop, but any digital software can be used to
create the works in this book. I will be using an on-screen drawing tablet throughout. You will get better results using an on-screen tablet, but I have done these
exercises before using an off-screen tablet and also a mouse in the past. You may
also choose to use paper and marker pens, if digital technology isn't available.

Before we start getting into the tasks and how we start to build images, I will
just go through a couple of important starting pointers when it comes to working
digitally and the important features in Photoshop. Photoshop is a massive piece of
software, but we will be using a very, very small amount of its features.

Choosing canvas size.

DOI: 10.1201/9781003500032-5

When you first load up Photoshop or any other digital programme for that matter, you will be asked for canvas size. This is where you will lay down all your marks when building images. For studies and practicing painting any size is fine, but if your computer can handle it then choose a size around the 2000 width mark. For the work I do I tend to work at 3300 by 2550 Pixels.

Blank canvas to start.

Once you have your canvas, on either side of the screen you will have your tools, brushes, etc. On the left of your canvas, you have brushes and options. With layers and how you apply them on your right. Above are drop down bars for everything else. This can all sound terrifying, but we will only be working with about 5% of this, so don't worry.

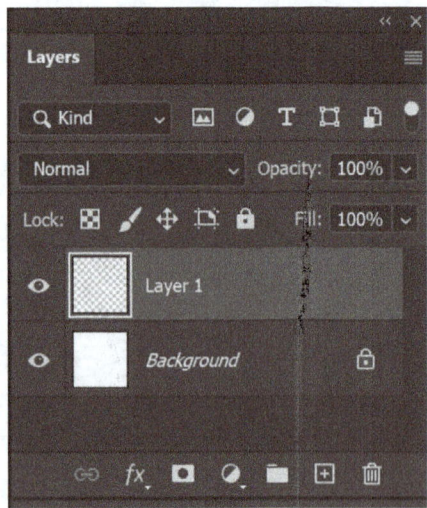

Layers side menu.

You can use the plus icon in the bottom right corner to add layers to your document. Layers enable you to structure your images and marks on top of one another. And this is done through simply dragging the layer above and below to the desired place in the stack.

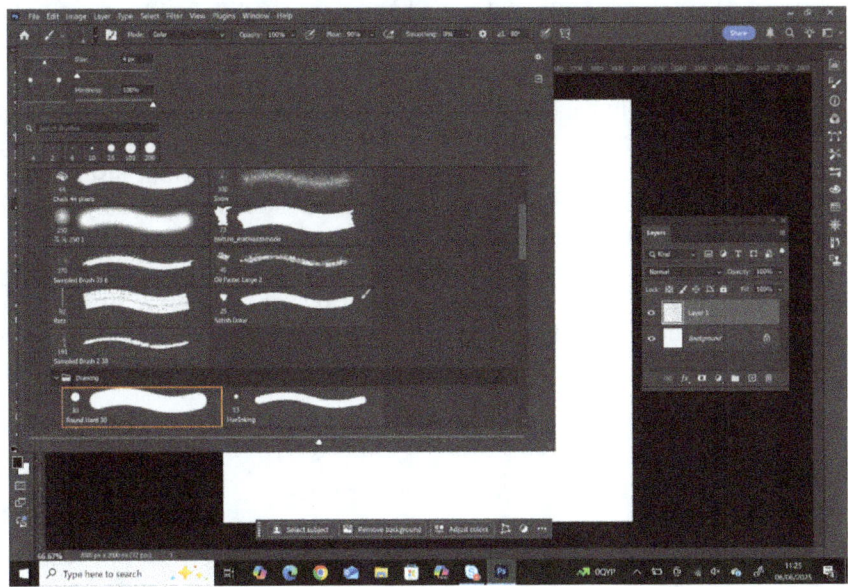

Brushes to choose from.

If you choose the brush from the left hand tool bar, you are then able to select the brush preset picker where your brushes are housed. There are lots of great free brushes and legacy brushes available, and all of these will help you get started.

After this you are now pretty much ready to start putting marks on the digital canvas. The only other thing to know, at this stage is the Tilder key. This is on your keyboard and is the one below the escape key in the top left. The Tilder key I use more than any other and it allows you to use the brush that you are using to paint as an eraser. This will save you a bunch of time and is my preferred way to work.

DRAWING VS PAINTING

First of all, it's worth talking a little about two of the techniques we will be using to create our works, environment studies, characters and pieces of concept art in general. Drawing and painting represent the two primary ways that we can visualise as artists and designers. Both of these techniques are taught to us in childhood and are instinctive ways of communicating. This is great in terms of our familiarity with these techniques because they need little description. However, our expectation for what we can create using drawing and painting far out strips our actual ability if we are just starting out.

Drawing and painting are two very different processes and require two different mindsets as a designer/artist.

Drawing and painting I see as two different tools used to represent objects and the worlds we create. Drawing is the process of the marking out of the parameters of the thing you are trying to create. Whereas painting is the blocking out of shapes and masses that build up the image as a whole.

Both of these techniques have their strengths and weaknesses, in terms of their ease of use and application. Neither is better or worse than the other. We will all use these specific techniques for different situations. But just remember, these are tools and the more tools you have, the more options you have for problem solving in the images you create.

Below is the way I create an environment using both drawing and painting separately. I have set up to produce two variations of the picture below. One using drawing and one using painting. Both will be quick 10-minute versions of the scene.

Classic British countryside.

I begin with a rough line sketch of the major landmarks in the scene. These are really simple and are there to represent the environment.

I then start to use lines to flesh out and add slightly more detail within the environment and also start to add value to show light and dark.

Painting and drawing of this classic British field.

The result of both techniques is very different and can be used situationally depending on the need. Play around with these two ways of working and if you find yourself stuck and unable to solve a problem then alternate these two techniques in and out.

WHERE I USE DRAWING AS A TECHNIQUE

I used to use drawing as my primary technique when I was designing and building any form of concept art, whether that be environment or character. I think the main reason for this is familiarity with pencil and paper. I am from the generation who grew up without Photoshop or any other digital painting tools, such as tablets or even search engines. When I was younger, I also tended to draw, as opposed to painting when I was trying to create something. Drawing was always a fairly readably available tool when I was growing up. I always carried a sketchbook with me wherever I went (and still do), which was great, if I saw something that struck me, like a landscape or a person, I could just open up my bag, grab out my sketchbook and pencil and start drawing.

One of the other major reasons why sketching was my go-to technique was because we were taught to draw by my tutors and teachers. I never really got painting at that time, it seemed messy, less instinctual and not as flexible as drawing.

At some point after an accumulation of Art School and freelance design jobs, being exposed to photoshop, drawing tablets and research I started to use digital painting to block out as a primary visualisation tool. This became a bit of a game changer for me and my work. I soon realised that I could use drawing to problem solve in certain situations but also use digital where drawing was problematic.

WHERE I USE PAINTING AS A TECHNIQUE

Painting or blocking out is the primary way I prefer to design out environments and characters. The way that I start with painting is by building the big masses of, either the environment or character first, using a large opaque brush and then shrinking the brush I am using down gradually, for more medium and smaller details as I need. This method requires me to establish the big shapes of the thing I am creating as accurately as possible first and then using this as a thing to build off of, and use as reference for the other shapes I paint in.

Drawing doesn't really occur in the painting process for me until I need to start mapping out the internal detail of the shapes I have created. What I mean by this is, when I have a rough mass or shape to represent an object I will decide if these needs defining. If I am working on a character and feel that there is some internal detail that needs showing. I will quickly draw that in with linework to show the shape of the image.

Two samurai's two techniques.

Two examples of the benefits and results of painting and drawing in character concept art.

WHERE I USE DRAWING AND PAINTING AS A TECHNIQUE

I have used drawing and painting together in the past and I sometimes combine both of these techniques, depending on the situation. I use these two techniques together usually on things like complex non-organic environments. Cities, streets, industrial areas, that kind of thing. This applies to both interior, as well as exterior settings. I don't often use this technique for characters or props, but that is down to personal preference. There are, however, lots of exceptional characters and prop artists who work using sketching and painting. If you are starting out, I would just use whatever feels right for the specific situation you are in. If a painting or drawing is causing you consistent problems, it might be worth trying out another way of working for the thing that is causing you problems. It's important to remember that drawing, painting and a hybrid of the two are just techniques and familiarity with these will lead to a better understanding of how to use them in your work and process.

DRAWING AND SKETCHING

For me drawing and sketching are almost the same thing, and for some artists they are. However, I see a subtle distinction between the two. In my process, I see sketching as an exploratory technique, used to rapidly produce ideas and concepts. These sketches are loose and are quick ways of getting an idea down on paper or screen.

Drawing is a little bit more finished and is almost like an advanced sketch. I often build on top of a sketch, really nail down the focal points and build it into a finished design through an iterative process.

Both these ways of working, sketching and drawing are different for every artist and can change depending on the product or brief that you are working on. At the end of the day these techniques or disciplines are just processes to get you to better artwork and designs.

OBSERVATIONAL DRAWING

Observational drawing is the exercise of observing an object and drawing it, it's that simple. This is a common practice on arts-based courses in education and is a really good way of getting better at visualising in its most general terms.

Classic fruit bowl.

Drawing an object in a space is subtlety different from a still life drawing composition that we will go through below.

The most common way that this exercise is taught is through still life drawing. This is where we take, usually a collection of objects, arrange them and then draw them. The excellent thing about this exercise is that it tests the essence of what it means to visually communicate. There are variations to this task that open up other interesting drawing experiences and we will go through some of them below.

STILL LIFE

Still life refers to the act of drawing and painting staged inanimate objects in an organised composition. These objects are usually set up on a plinth or table in an interesting way to draw or paint. This activity has been used for generations as a way of developing visualisation and observational tools. This exercise I did many years ago, regularly, while at art school, and is a session I run a couple of times a year with my current students. There are many variations you can do whilst drawing and we will go through some of them in the tasks below.

Fruit bowl with company.

For this task, we are going to do a series of still life sessions. We are going to start out with a standard session and then move onto more experimental one, designed to test different areas of drawing and thinking. That's right drawing and thinking. It's important to remember that mastering any exercise is as much about the thinking behind the process, as much as it is about the process itself. We will learn more about this as we get to the exercises.

Task: Still life drawing

Curated fruit arrangement.

A STANDARD SESSION OF STILL LIFE DRAWING

For this first session, you will need the following things:

- Arrange some objects on a table in an interesting composition.
- Pencil, pen and pad or digital drawing equipment (Ipad, drawing tablet).
- Plane backdrop so there is nothing to distract you behind the object you are drawing.
- Sit at least a meter or so away from the object(s).
- Set yourself a 15–20-minute timer and start to draw the object(s).

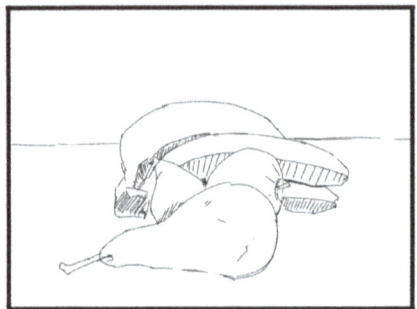 

Trying to underdo the sketch.

As long as your gestures lead to marks that capture the essence of the thing you are drawing then you should be alright.

Task: Alternative still life drawing sessions

These alternative sessions follow the same rules as the traditional drawing session. You are still just drawing the thing in front of you but using a different technique or restriction to facilitate a different way to draw. The purpose of these alternative still life drawing sessions is not to end up with an amazing, finished drawing. It's to make your brain engage differently. So, when doing one of these sessions don't worry about the end product, just enjoy the process.

- Choose one object that you have just drawn.
- 10–20 minutes to draw or paint the scene.
- Draw the scene with your weaker hand.
- Draw the scene with your eyes closed.
- Draw the scene without taking your pencil off the page or screen.

Chapter 6

Environment concept art

ENVIRONMENT CONCEPT ART OVERVIEW

Environmental concept art is the imagining and creating of worlds/environments, usually for games, film and television. A concept artists biggest asset is their ability to imagine new and interesting things and tell stories through the things they create. This process starts with a brief defining the project. A concept artists will then research around the subject area, both visually and non-visually. This part is important if there is unfamiliarity with the subject area. It's even more important to research if you are familiar with the subject area. Knowing too much about a particular subject can lead artists to fall into genre tropes and tread already trodden ground. So, finding a new way to approach an unfamiliar and familiar subject is paramount for any visual artist. Once an idea has formulated in the artist's head, they will begin visualising the environment. This is done through drawing and painting, putting as many ideas as possible onto the page or screen. Iteration is the key to finding the best designs and this can only happen if you try things out. Once you have a bunch of ideas, your lead will give feedback and there may be amendments to particular designs resulting in detail passes on your work, followed by a finished product in the form of either a detailed value or colour painting. This is a bit of an oversimplification but generally speaking this is a typical breakdown of creating environment concept art.

Concept artists at their core are problem solvers. Concept artists need to be able to come up with ideas and visualise them rapidly because of the fast passed nature of the creative sector. The worlds that a concept artist build for games, film or television need to engage the player or viewer on multiple levels. This is a really tricky task and the process itself is designed to focus their energy on options and not too much detail in the early phase of production. Only after a clear visual style is established for an environment that sets the scene, will production then forward.

SHAPE OR SILHOUETTE

Shape for me is the most important consideration when painting and designing environment concept art (and character). From my perspective, shape and silhouette are indistinguishable and represent the same thing what we talk

DOI: 10.1201/9781003500032-6

about them. So, when I am talking about shape and shape design just know I am referring to the silhouette of the object as well.

The eyes make the statue look more sinister than it was.

Even the most complex objects in the world can be broken down into simple shapes that are understood at a glance.

What is the simplest symbol that best describes the shape.

Robb Rupple, Graphic L.A.

Shape is the space that an object or thing within the environment occupies. This can be anything from clouds, buildings, rocks, people, shadows, lakes, anything. The most important thing to remember is that these shapes are abstract. This is one of the key areas that beginner artists struggle with. The main reason for this is because of how our brains are programmed to work. Our brains are always wanting to simplify the things we draw and paint down and be understood by the people looking at them. Let's take, for example, trees. We see trees all the time in the world around us and these are also very common objects in pieces of environmental concept art. The problem that beginners face while painting them is, rather than painting what their tree reference looks like, they tend to fall into the trap of drawing the symbol version of a tree. The reason for this difference is because of our brains desire to simplify and communicate. This is a really common thing to have happen and a fairly straightforward thing to sort out.

The way to solve this problem is trust your eye and not your brain. What I mean by this is when painting or drawing a tree, for instance, use your reference. Draw or paint the shapes that you see and not what you imagine. It's really common for beginner artists to have reference in front of them and not understand what they are trying to communicate. Our brain will see the tree reference, for instance, and will disconnect. It will think *"Ahhh, I know what you are trying to draw, a tree, let me take over"* and this is what leads to the symbol of a tree or the thing you are trying to draw/paint.

The thing is your brain isn't wrong, it is a tree that you are trying to communicate, it's just not your tree and this is the most important distinction. Paint your version of things, not your brains, and how we do this is through the shape we draw and paint.

Classic tree and an imagined version of this.

If we look the tree above as our example, it looks fairly ordinary and it's easy to see how a beginner artist could look at it and end up with a drawing like the one above.

Classic tree now taking shape.

And if I was going to paint the tree reference above, I would actually start with an initial painting that is very similar. The difference being however that I wouldn't stop there. I would continue to look back and forth at the reference and make sure the rough masses and distinguishing features of this particular tree are represented in my version.

Tree shape now defined through shape detail.

After I convey the specific, simple characteristics of the reference, it is just the case of looking at the medium and small details and conveying them. If you get most of the big masses right, it is just a case of erasing the parts you don't need.

Shape is something that beginner artists really sleep on, and they shouldn't. The shape of an object is the most important thing in terms of communication and how we see the world. If the underlying shape of an object is wrong or incorrect, the whole image will fall apart and not communicate the thing you want it to. The way we paint shapes defines the structure of the objects we design, so it's easy to see how important this process is in communicating ideas.

There are a number of exercises to help with how you develop your shape language, and we will dig into some of them now.

SHAPE DETAIL

Shape detail refers to the amount of detail the silhouette of an object has. I would say as a general rule, try to make sure the work you produce is readable first, before adding detail to the silhouette. What I mean by this is can someone understand what the thing is at a glance? If they can, that's great, you now might want to add a little more detail to the silhouette.

How detailed this needs to be really does depend on what stage of the design process you are at. If you are really early on and are just generating ideas and producing iterations, there is less need to have very considered, detailed silhouettes. I have found that focusing on shape and relying on this to tell the story of the object leads to better results.

Thinking about every shape in your environment as abstract, is the key to freeing up your process and building better work.

One of the ways of simplifying the world around you is by squinting, while looking at objects and the things around you.

The best way to understand how shape/silhouette works within painting and environment design is to paint something. I have found that there are a number of things to ease you into the painting process. The best way to start is to paint an irregular object or something with organic shapes. Rocks, bones, trees and sculptures are really good places to start, if you are a beginner. Things like buildings, cars, humans and precision manmade objects, etc, are designed and are difficult to paint if you are starting out. So, stay away from these difficult objects when starting out.

As stated above, the best places to start when drawing and painting is with irregular objects like bones, rocks and trees. The best part about these types of objects is that they are irregular, and if you get parts wrong, it is harder to see and if you are starting out, taking the pressure off yourself will help you enjoy the process more and get you an easy win.

Task: Drawing and painting rocks

We are now going to use some visual reference to paint and draw some rocks.

The main reason we start by practicing drawing and painting rocks and other organic objects is because they have an achievable shape and there is wiggle room to make mistakes. It's a relatively easy win, which is great at this stage.

- Find five reference pictures of rocks or use the link below.
- Draw out the five rocks.
- Paint out the same five rocks.
- Avoid detailing.
- Take about 10 minutes for each one.

You can source your own reference pictures or use the ones in the linked Pinterest pages.

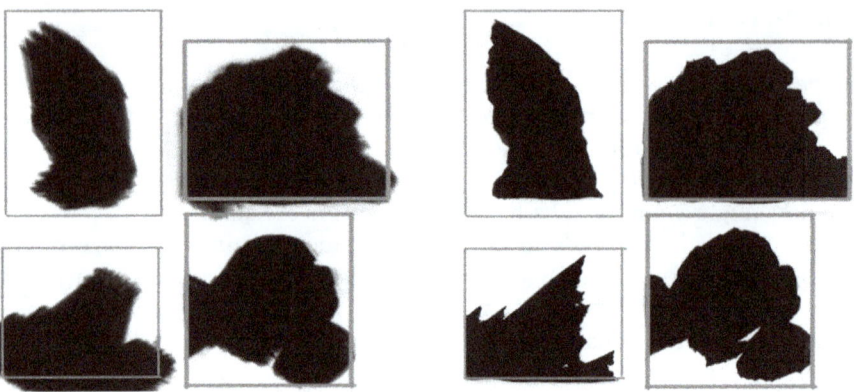

Getting the big rock shapes right first. Refining the rock shapes next.

The first step is to capture the simple shape of the rocks (left). Then refine these to a more accurate shape (Right).

I start by establishing the simple statement or rough shape (left). Then I carve the rough shape (right). I keep looking back and forth to my reference to get it as accurate as possible.

To start with look at the shape of the object. Now use a simple brush to paint in the shape of the rock. Don't worry about detail, this stage is all about getting the underlaying shape down and making sure you can transform what you see to digital paper.

As you work through this, just use simple adding and subtracting to make sure the shape of the rock is replicated. Try to use as big a brush as possible at this early blocking out phase. Then scale your brush down as you get into the finer details of the shape and its edges.

https://www.pinterest.co.uk/lees0301/rocks/

Task: Two value rocks

In the next task, we are going to tackle adding value detail to the rocks you have just painted. For this, it is important that you really look at the reference you used to paint the rocks out. We are going to use this reference to add high and low lights to the rock silhouettes. To do this, we need to make a decision as to where the light and dark areas are on the rock, as well as where we want to show detail.

- Use the existing rocks you have just painted.
- Really look at the reference images you are using.
- Take about 10 minutes for each painting.
- Add a clipping mask to the layer with the rock you are painting.
- Don't be scared to try things out.

Simple shape of the rock first. Using value to add detail to the shape.

TREES

Another great exercise to cut your teeth on as a beginner artist is drawing and painting trees. These big recognisable organic shapes are a great place to start the drawing and painting process.

For this next task, we are now going to use visual reference to draw and paint out some trees. We will do this in the same way we did with rocks task.

Firstly, lets grab five tree reference images of the trees you want to draw out and five reference images for trees you want to paint out. Try to grab trees that have distinct foliage and shape to them. Try not to grab references of trees with intricate branches. The reason for this is it will take a very long time to draw out every branch and a very short time to draw distinct canopies. Drawing out branches and tiny details is something that at this stage we don't need to focus on, that main area we want to focus on is just drawing and painting big shapes accurately.

Task: Drawing out trees

We are now going to draw these trees out.

- Choose five trees from the reference link provided.
- Draw out the trees.
- Focus mainly on the overall shape of the trees you are drawing.
- Take around 20 minutes per sketch.

The next task we are going to do is painting trees. We are going to focus on just the shape of the tree and capturing the silhouette. We will work the same way we did on the last task, big shapes first and only focusing on the detail of the shape as we paint. No internal detail.

Task: Painting out trees

We are now going to paint the trees you have chosen out.

- Choose five trees from the reference link provided.
- Paint out the trees.
- Focus mainly on the overall shape of the trees you are painting.
- Use a big brush to cover large areas.
- Take around 20 minutes per painting.

You can source your own reference pictures or use the ones in the linked Pinterest pages.

https://www.pinterest.co.uk/lees0301/trees/

For this painting task, I have chosen two different trees to paint. I have deliberately chosen two contrasting pictures to do studies from. The first is a tree lacking in detail, it has an easy to see silhouette. The second is a far more detailed tree with lots of branches and a complex silhouette.

Full trees are great to paint when starting out. Trees without leaves will take more time and are more complex.

Both of these trees should be started in exactly the same way and avoid the little details.

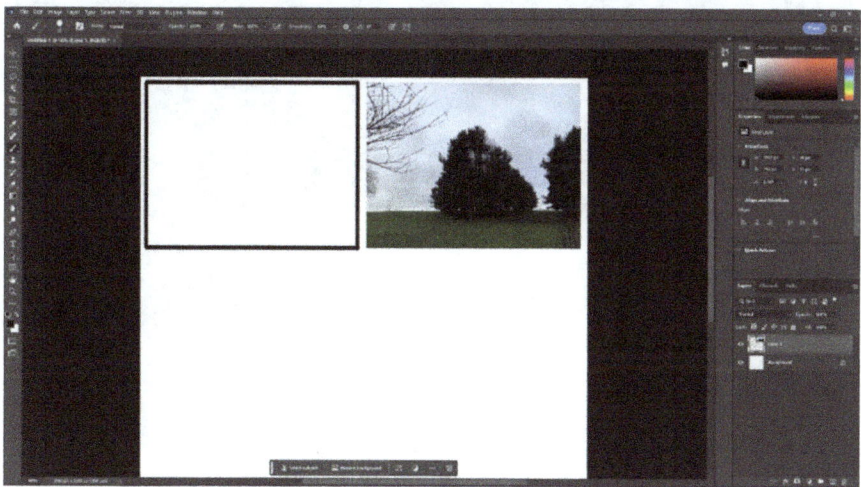

Before painting and imaging where the tree would sit.

I make sure I imagine where the marks are going to go before they get placed.

The blobs are in the right place.

Laying in the big masses and rough shapes is the key to a successful end product.

Using the shape to carve into to reveal a tree shape.

Then, rough carving of the initial shapes shows the next level of detail and even if we left it there, that would be enough.

Further tree carving and establishing fine detail.

Adding a few more details and some internal amendments is all the image needs.

The next tree that we will be painting for this study is a very different proposition, the reason I chose this tree is because of its variety of detail.

Lots of detail to paint here.

I keep the approach for this tree the same as the previous one, imagine where things will sit on the canvas.

Initial rough lines placed.

Big shapes and accurate placement is my primary aim at the start.

Random controlled detail makes the tree.

The detail is a bit of a facard, I don't place down every branch, that could take twice as long and end up in a very similar end result. I put marks down from a distance with a smaller brush to get the feel of the tree right. This way of working can be applied to everything you draw and paint, so try to use this in your work.

Chapter 7

Value

THE VALUE OF VALUE

Value without question is one of the most important fundamentals that you need to be aware of and learn when it comes to concept art and being able to communicate visually. Value refers to how light or dark something is.

Even though our eyes see the world around us in colour, value is a core structure that underpins this. Everything we see has a value, when we see shadows in the world around us, these would be represented by dark values were we to paint them. When we look at a bright sky during the day we would be using light values if we were painting. All of this is subject specific however, if we were looking at shadows on dark overcast day, they may well be a medium value, depending on what the environment was that we were in. This applies to the lighter values as well. The night sky may well be a dark value if the moon is in the sky. So, it's important that you use your eyes, best judgement and instinct. One of the keyways to get your head around this is if you look at a photo on your phone. By turning it to black and white you aren't fundamentally changing the structure of photo just taking the colour away. Value is just a simplified way of seeing the world and we can use this principle in how we use value to paint and draw.

Value is also a key component in how we create visual interest in the works we create. I like to imagine value a stripped back easier way of seeing the world around us.

Take a concentrated amount of time to learn value and how to use it. The amount of detail you can get into your designs with just value is incredible. This also means you are working quicker because you aren't stressing about colour and the relationships of colours. Meaning you will be producing more images and idea in the long run. Working in just value is a real game changer and is as close as you are going to find to a magic bullet for your work.

DOI: 10.1201/9781003500032-7

VALUE SLIDER

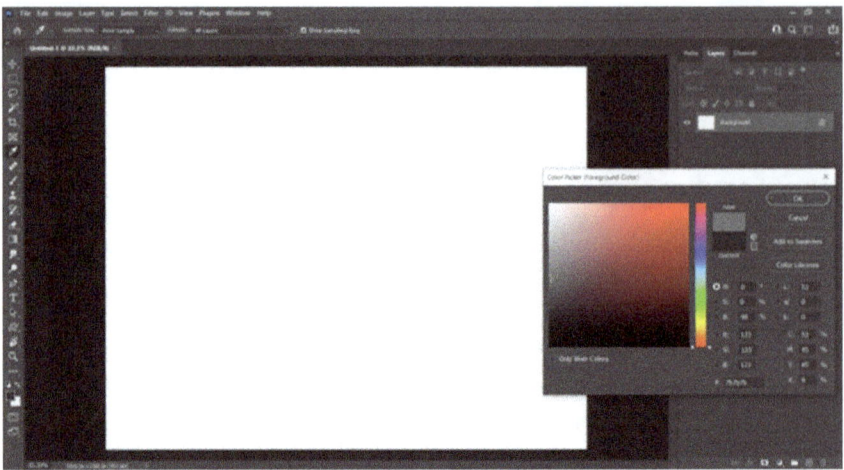

Value is much easier than colour to build with.

Above you can see across the left-hand side of the drop down bar the value scale. This is an indication of how light or dark the value is that you select.

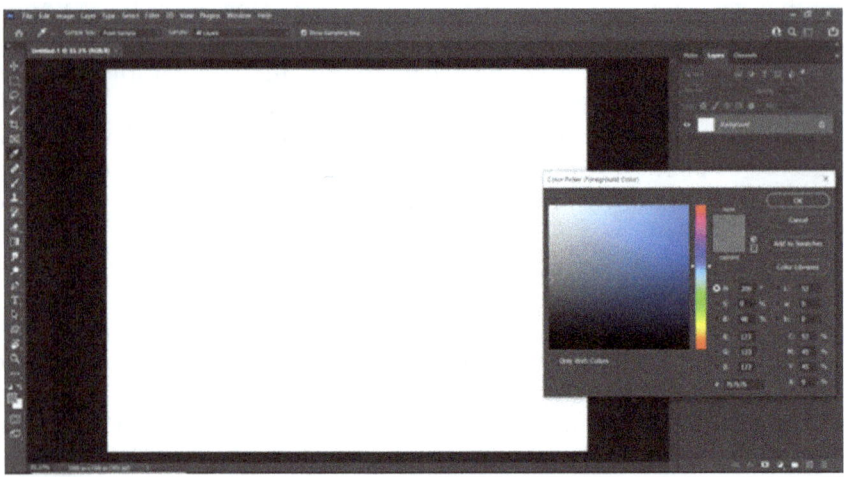

Colour may change but value stays the same.

When it comes to colour, this is located anywhere to the right of the far left-hand side. As you move up and down on the colour picker, the colour changes and also does the value. Higher is lighter and lower is darker.

COLOUR SLIDER

Value is one of the most important processes that I learned while at art school. It was something I totally underestimated at the time, and it was only years later while working as a storyboard/concept artist that I realised how important it was in the creation of images.

The biggest benefit of value is that it enables you to simplify the things you draw down into manageable chunks. If we take the pictures below as an example, both are understandable and all the things in the scene are visible and even the tone of the picture is readable. The only difference is colour.

Colour ducks. Black and white ducks.

Both colour and black and white images are recognisable and not a huge amount is lost from colour to black and white.

If we look at the colour picker below, you will see that the whole range of values is in the black and white ranges are down the left-hand side of the screen. So, we can select any value from black (at the bottom) to white (at the top), and all the shades of grey in between. Even on just this scale, the amount of choice is enormous. If we then look at colour and in particular the shades of red on the screen, we can see the variety of options that there is, even just in the red spectrum. It's infinitely bigger than the whole range of values. If we then take every colour available and the variety that's available within all these colours, you will see the problem artists facing. So, let's simplify this by just focusing on value. This will change the way you work, and you don't need to sacrifice detail.

When working in value, there is an option for the artist to choose how many different shades they use. This scale ratchets up and down depending on how complex and detailed you want the image to be. The lower the amount of values, the simpler the image. The more values the more detailed and harder the image will be to construct and paint.

Value shows as much detail as colour. Colour is huge.

Tip: When working in value, try to not work in pure black and white when painting. Work in dark grey and light grey.

VALUE RANGE

When creating a landscape or piece of environment concept art, the image itself has a range of values. These values control the mood and feel of the piece. This is what is referred to as the value range. The easiest way to break this down is using the 80/20 rule. 80% of the image is light or dark depending on what mood or atmosphere that you are wanting to create. With 20% being the opposite of this.

So, for example…

Mainly darks create an uneasy mood.

Above is a quick Notan breakdown of the stone, trees and path in the picture. If we look at it in terms of pure values (from a painting perspective), we can see that about 70–80% of the photo is in the dark value range. Inherently, the image has contrast, because of the imbalance in overall values.

This is why the image works.

 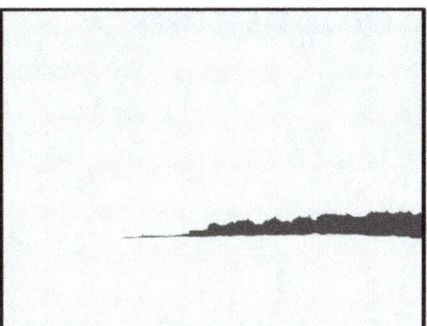

Mainly lights create a hopeful mood.

The image above is the inverse of the previous photo, with 80% of the image being light values. Again, this is what creates the contrast in the image, the imbalance. Both of these images represent a really good strategy when it comes to designing concept environments.

Chapter 8

Composition

INTRODUCTION TO COMPOSITION

Composition is the arrangement of objects and elements within a scene.

Composition is one of the major considerations when designing environments and environment concept art. There are many elements to what makes up composition, as it relates to environment, and it can seem overwhelming but once you have a grasp of the basics, it is a little more digestible.

Below is a list of what I see as the major elements to consider when designing compositions:

- Play space
- Rule of Thirds
- Foreground, midground and background
- Contrast
- Mixture of shapes

Where you place objects and how you arrange them in the world can have a massive impact on the viewer. In concept art for games and film, everything in the scene is important and is there to help tell a story and set the scene as well as the mood of the piece. It can be difficult to know where to start with composition, especially when it comes to your own work. The best place to start in my opinion is by looking at the work that got you interested in concept art in the first place.

Composition also applies to character, but we will go through that when we get to designing characters.

PLAY SPACE

Another consideration that needs to be thought about when building concept art for games and film is the play space. The play space refers to the area in a game that the player plays in. In a film of television show, this would refer to anything you are able to see in a scene. Now this is a very important consideration for concept artists. In early production for games and film, there will

DOI: 10.1201/9781003500032-8

be very little built for a concept artist to work from. So, the concept artist will be partly responsible for not just designing the look of the intellectual property (IP) but also the player–viewers interactions in and with the space. What I mean by this is a concept artist needs to consider the player and viewer in their design process:

- Where they place objects in the scene?
- What is the player or character doing in the space?
- What part of the story are we in?
- How do you want them to feel?
- What can I put in the space to help tell the story?

These are just some of the considerations that need to be thought of in the design process.

LEVEL OF DETAIL

Generally speaking, a concept artists job is to come up with ideas and visualise them so that they are understood. Most of the time a simple, clear drawing or painting will do this, and it can usually be built in the future or as the project moves forward. This clarity of image is often misunderstood by beginner artists. This clarity doesn't mean the fidelity of your image or the amount of detail that your work shows. It is simply, does my image convey the information I need? Often a good silhouette drawing or painting with good shape design is enough to communicate this. But beginner artists sometimes judge how well something is rendered, as to whether the piece is successful or not. What usually happens is beginner artists often forget about how important shape and value is within their work and end up in an endless loop of adding things to their work. This then leads to them not being able to get away from the unnecessary bits they have just created, making it harder to see how to correct this. It is really hard to "kill your darlings", as the saying goes. Especially when you have worked really hard on something. But this needs to be done if compositionally the piece you have created doesn't work and fails to communicate your intentions.

The main things to remember is scaffold your work with simple, readable shape, followed by clear values and composition. These are two guides or philosophies to try and embed in your work. But the best place to start is by trying things out.

RULE OF THIRDS

The Rule of Thirds is a mechanism and structure used to devise interesting compositions and images. This Rule of Thirds refers to dividing up your compositions into nine equal segments. Where these segments intersect is where you should consider placing focal points or areas of interest for the viewer.

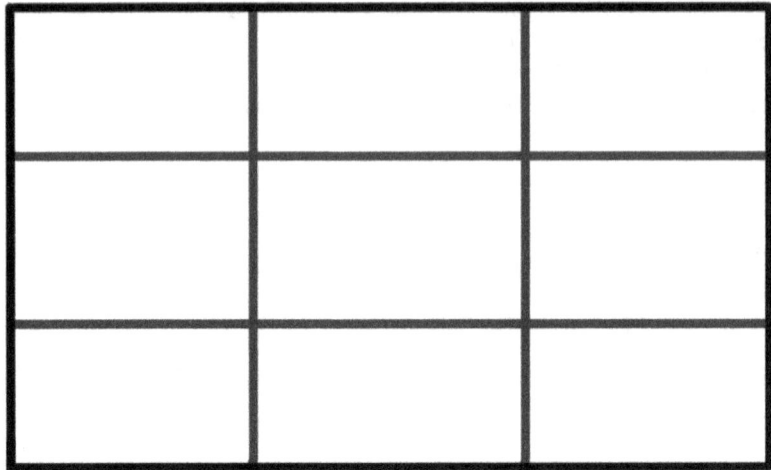

Rule of Thirds grid.

Example of the Rule of Thirds grid used to find compositions.

I wouldn't necessarily call this a rule perse, but it is certainly a good thing to have in mind as you design compositions, especially if you are just starting out.

There are also things like the Fibonacci/Golden Spiral, which can be used in the same way as the Rule of Thirds, by placing objects of significance in specific areas of the spiral to create pleasing compositions and images. The Fibonacci/Golden Spiral is found all through nature and has been used by artists through the ages.

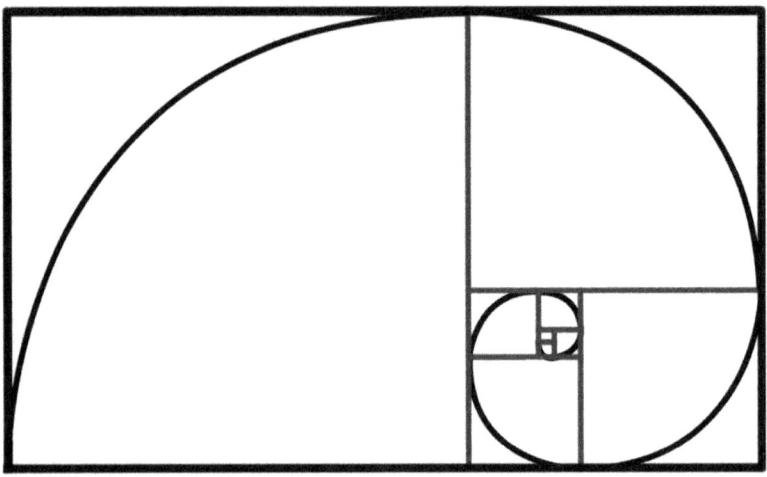

Fibonacci Spiral.

Example of the Golden Ratio or Fibonacchi Spiral used to find compositions.

Below is an example picture of a landscape I took while visiting a place in Northumberland. I have placed this picture underneath the Rule of Thirds example and the Golden Ratio example, to show how we could use this in real terms.

Classic composition to paint from.

We will use this castle to show how the Rule of Thirds and the Golden Ratio work.

If we were painting something similar to the image above or indeed any landscape piece, it can be quite hard to make decisions on where objects sit in the space you are designing. This is where the Rule of Thirds or the Golden Ratio could help.

As you can see by the overlay below, placing the castle across the first two middle segments enables the surrounding segments to frame the castle with the fence posts, sky, grass and trees. All of this contributing to a strong overall composition.

Focal points are easier to see when using a grid.

We can see the main areas of interest fall close to the cross sections on the grid.

For the Golden Ratio overlay I just flipped the Golden Ratio guide vertically, to match the castle in the scene. This is an important thing to remember when using the Golden Ratio, it can be used in any orientation to suite your composition. We can see when this is placed on the image that the open spiral on the right-hand side is an area of rest within the structure of the image. And this matches perfectly with the surroundings of the image. Every image you create needs areas of rest, and this adds to the contrast inherent within your images Detail v's non detail.

Areas of rest towards the end of the spiral.

The tight curves of the spiral converge exactly where the castle is.

I would say that all of these methods are excellent tools, but I wouldn't stick to them rigidly on every piece of work you build. Try to find what works for you and your work, but by all means use these tools as a guide, particularly if you draw or paint an environment and you can't put your finger on what to change.

FOREGROUND MIDGROUND AND BACKGROUND

Designing and building a piece of environment concept art can be really daunting or confusing, especially where to start. The empty canvas can cause even the most seasoned artist problems. When looking at the reference you are using for inspiration, there are things everywhere which can lead to confusion. So, take a step back, think and try to simplify.

Clear fore, mid and backgrounds.

All environments can be broken down into foreground, midground and background.

One way of breaking this space down is through breaking your frame up into your foreground, midground and background. You don't physically have to do this, but it can be really helpful.

Foreground refers to the area closest to the camera (where we are looking from and the closest elements).

Foreground.

Midground refers to the area between the foreground and background (the areas that sit just before the background).

Foreground, midground.

The background refers to the area right at the back and off into the distance (this will include usually the sky and areas in the far distance).

Foreground, midground and background.

Below is a really good breakdown of this by Sparth, a concept artist, who has worked on the Halo games series. He does a really excellent job of explaining the nuances of his workflow in relation to creating environment concept pieces.
https://www.youtube.com/watch?v=H6HZuGjCcgQ

CONTRAST

Contrast is the arrangement of opposites to create areas of interest and conflict.
Contrast is a vital tool in the artist/designer's toolbox and covers a large area of different elements within a drawing, painting or piece of concept art.
Here are some of the areas that contrast covers:

- Big and small
- Light or dark
- Hard or soft
- Detailed or undetailed
- Finished or unfinished
- Sharp or round
- Busy and not busy

These areas of contrast are used by all concept artists and can make a big impact to your work, as well as on the viewer. All the examples listed above can, and should be used across environments and character concept art, to elevate your work and help your work communicate with the person looking at it.

The first two areas of contrast on this list that I want to cover are, big and small and light and dark. For me these are your primary ways of communicating with your viewer and represent the most important two types of contrast to me and the way I work. That isn't to say the other forms or contrast aren't important, it just means it's almost impossible to create piece of visual work or piece of concept art without them. The other forms of contract both on the list and others that I might have missed, are what I would considered primarily to enhance an image, not establishing it, the flavour if you will.

The first type of contrast I tend to focus on, is big or small, and I do this through shape design, as talked about earlier in this book. Shape is the tool that every other element relies on and is our primary communication tool. Without defining the shape, you will really struggle to define any of the other elements. Shape is the foundation and frame that holds our work together. I can't emphasise this enough. You can communicate so much information just through the shape and silhouette of an object, environment or character alone.

Dark chair shape.

The shape of this chair above communicates lots on information, even with no internal detail.

Once you have defined what the shape of the object or objects is, i.e., how large or small it is and what shape it occupies in the space or world that it exists in. I now tend to focus on value. For me, shape and value tend to go hand in hand and are the fundamental building blocks of visual communication.

The use of value is what I would call instant contrast. This means that as long as you are using at least two different values, you are always going to get some form of value contrast in your work. In its simplest form, the greater the difference in value (light or dark) the heavier the contrast. Combining these first two elements of shape (large–small) and value (light–dark) will be the thing that holds your work together.

Highlights on the chair.

Just a few touches of contrast added to the chair shape can instantly transform the shape into something a little more complex. As stated before, the more values you add the more complex the image becomes.

Once you have the shape and value in place, I iterate and play around with the placement of these shapes to try and find the best composition for the thing I am trying to create. I then look at some of the other ways of creating contrast from the list above (sharp or round, busy or not busy, etc.) to best create the tone for what I am trying to create. The thought process for character and environment is slightly different from each other. However, the underlying principles of both these two different types of design remain very similar, as do the fundamentals that underpin them and are all essential if you want to create interesting engaging works.

MIXTURE OF SHAPE SIZES

In environment and character design, the way you design and organise your shapes can transform an average image into something much more interesting. Creating images that tell stories and engage the viewer/player on an emotional level should be the aim as visual artists.

One good rule that I like to follow and bleed into the way I work, is making sure you have a good mixture of large, medium and small shapes. This arrangement and distribution of a good mixture of shapes can really help sell a believable environment/character. It is possible, and in some cases necessary to have things that exist in the environment and on a character that have similar size shapes. For example, a desert with small rocks or an open field would be a good example of a space containing mainly small shapes. On a character you might have small repeating shapes like buttons on a jacket or bullets in a bandoleer, which are very similar to each other.

A good example of mainly large shapes would be if you were inside a forest with large looming trees. But within these spaces you would still find some counter points to these shapes, for example, in a forest you might have small bushes and branches or patches of grass, even rocks and flowers. So just be careful with using too many similar shapes.

Naturally, when painting, we tend to paint everything as a medium shape. This tends to lead to paintings looking flat and lifeless. The human brain loves to organise and spot patterns, and this is one of the main reasons beginner artists tend to end up with lots of medium shapes and a very ordered environment/character. This environment/character will inevitably look sterile and lacking in visual interest if there isn't any variation in your shape design. Although eradicating shapes that look too similar in terms of their size should be something to look out for, the important part is that you see and spot them in your work. You should then look at how you can change these shapes to create more visual interest and contrast in the works that we create.

OVERLAP

Overlap is the term used to describe any object that you draw or paint that is overlapping another object. This is used in art and concept art to create depth, a degree of realism and visual storytelling.

The use of overlap in the environments and characters you will create is vital if you want to build works that have depth, variety and visual interest.

If you look at the world around you, overlap is everywhere and is the natural way we see the world.

Overlap isn't just a way to make environments/characters look believable, it is also a way to draw the viewers eye around an image you make, and to enhance the stories you tell.

RELATIVE SIZE

Relative size refers to the size of an object depending on where it is in the environment. This can add important depth cues to the work you create. I just remember it as the Farther Ted principle, the cow is bigger the closer it is to the person or camera, and smaller the further away it is. Relative size applies to everything, big or small. One thing beginner artist's get stuck on, is scaling things like mountains or trees, I think because of their general large size. People find it difficult to keep this in mind as they place large objects throughout their scenes.

A lone tree. Three trees.

If there is one object in an environment it is difficult to imagine how large it is. This tree could be three feet tall, or it could be 50 feet tall, we have no idea and no scale reference.

If we place more similar objects in the space, we can get a better sense of the size of the object we are looking at. And in this case, we can make some assumptions that something that looks like a tree is probably going to be tree size. However, if all the trees, in this case are an equal size it leads to a level of falseness in the image you are creating. If we look at any environment, trees are usually a mixture of different sizes and shapes.

Big, medium and small tree. Big medium and small tree moved.

Now if we change the size of these trees in the space, we create a greater level of believability in the image we are building. If we then move the trees around the space, we get an even higher level of believability in the spaces we build.

Big, medium and small overlapped.

The principle of relative size works really well with the overlapping principle we discussed in the previous chapter. Combining these two techniques together, overlapping relative sized objects is a great way to add depth and believability to your work.

I would always advise looking at real life environment when building imagined ones. This is a great way of making sure you are creating something that feels believable and keep this recognisable for the player or viewer.

> *Robb Rupple Graphic LA pg. 68 "Everything is an excuse to show depth, overlap, and form".*

> *Robb Rupple Graphic LA pg. 62 "When Sketching graphically from life, you have to alter the values to produce the design that makes the scene easiest to read and states the intent/focus".*

TANGENTS

Tangents are areas or objects that almost seem to touch within compositions. Most commonly this happens when you are painting or constructing objects in a scene. Tangents create a different kind of visual tension in your image and in most cases not in a good way. If these happen in your work unintentionally then try to either overlap the objects involved or move the objects further away from each other.

Some tangents are constructed on purpose. Take for instance, the Sisteen Chapel and the painting by Michelangelo. The tangent in the scene is where Adam and Gods fingers are almost touching. This creates a tension in the image that works and has become one of the most iconic images in art and wider culture.

When starting out I would try to spot and stay away from creating tangents and you may see them happen fairly frequently throughout your work. What you have to do is see them and change them, if they detract from your work and image.

The great hall.

Tangents create areas of visual conflict that can hurt an image, this applies to drawings, paintings and also photos.

If we were going to paint this image above, we would want to move these branches to create overlap. This overlap would create a move visually pleasing image for the viewer. We could also use this overlap with intent, and both draw the viewers eye to the arch, for story purposes or even to create an enticing visual atmosphere, if we were to overlap the branches across the stone arch and into the space itself.

Tangents.

The branches intersect with the arch, creating a subtle area of conflict for the viewer.

These tangents can happen organically in real life and can sometimes work in paintings but it's worth assessing if they detract from the image or scene and address them if they feel wrong.

FRAMING

Framing can refer to two different things within environment concept art. Firstly, this can refer to what you choose to put in your image and the boundary of your canvas.

It can however refer to the techniques used to keep the viewers eye inside the image. Using natural elements from the environment you are trying to create to keep the viewers eye inside the image and looking around. Typically, the things used to do this are trees or rocks and objects that are at the edge of the shot/canvas.

This holding of the viewers gaze can also apply to characters as well. The framing element in this case needs to be done through focal points on the character and how they are spread throughout the characters body. These framing elements could be hair, clothing, etc.

Tree gating in action.

In this extreme example, trees and branches frame the scene.

The trees and foliage in this case surround the boarders of the image creating nowhere for the viewer to look other than what is in the center of the image.

Red arrows in action.

The shapes you paint can be used to pull and push the viewers eye to where you want them to look.

When framing is used right, it not only deters the viewer from leaving the image but can also add to the story and tone of what is going on in the scene. In the case above, the framing focuses the attention of the viewer and the character in the scene on the gap in the wilderness. The branches at the top also help to convey the potential struggle the character might have been through, whilst also pointing the way out for the character.

Red arrows diving.

The verticals help to guide the viewer eye up and down to the areas of interest in the scene.

The verticals in the trees, path and smoke plumes all help to guide us to the character in the scene. All the areas of interest are located from lower left centre, where the character has come from, and then move outside right to inner high right, to illustrate where the character is headed. All of these subtle devises are great for storytelling and communicating visually with the viewer.

In the case of framing on characters, the framing elements became harder to see and far more mentally abstract than in environment work.

Stilt character.

The design of the character is in this case an "S" shape, designed to help the viewer move through the image.

We can see that the shape language used on this character pull the viewer around the image. The horns act as the catalyst for this and lead down to the arrow like objects, down to the ragged viny arms and to the spindle like legs. All of these shapes have a level of external detail to them which helps to communicate the importance to the viewer. This is then further enhanced by having a good blend of big, medium and small shapes for visual interest.

Reading the image.   Focal points.

Keeping the viewers eye on the character is done here through the design of the shapes pulling you through the image.

In this case, the internal detailing of focal points act as a framing mechanism to keep the viewers eyes on the character.

The internal white details are fairly sparce throughout the character and there are a number of reasons for this. The main reason is if I show the viewer vast amounts of detail imagination for the viewer goes out of the window. I want the person looking at this to have questions and want to know more. None of that will happen if I show them everything. I also don't want the viewer to stay in one place on the character for too long. So, less detail will keep the eye moving and circling back around, to try and find more information in the shapes.

GESTALT

Gestalt is the principle of seeing smaller objects as part of a bigger whole. We do this naturally in our daily lives all the time. One way to remember this is imagine looking at a field of long grass. Thousands upon thousands of individual strands of grass growing out from the ground. But when we see this (and draw/paint them) we see them as a field, or a block of colour rather than the individual blades of grass.

Environment gestalt.

We only need good shape design and values to trick the eye into thinking that the simplest shape is lots of complex ones.

This can apply to pretty much anything in an environment or on a character.

An example on a character might be hair or a beard. Thousands of hair of slightly different shades of colour but painted or drawn as relatively simple in shape and/or similar in colour.

Gestalt hair.

It doesn't have to be small objects either. Take a cityscape or view of a city from a distance. This view is made up of individual buildings, which in turn is made up of bricks, windows, etc. But when we see them, we don't see all these separate elements, only the buildings and cityscape as a whole.

All of these examples are very personal and context specific. What I mean by this is everybody's mind works differently, and everyone brings their own personal contexts and experiences to how they look at something. Someone who has a vested interest in architecture or building, may see a cityscape and see a collection of buildings, bricks and windows, instead of as a cityscape. But for most people this isn't the case.

This is one of the main principles that we can use as concept artists. It will really help speed up your process and will help you see the shape of object(s) rather than their internal detail.

Chapter 9

Storytelling

INTRODUCTION TO STORYTELLING

As humans we are always looking for stories in the media we consume. And we have always told stories, both visually and verbally for entertainment. One of the primary concerns for any concept artists is storytelling. How do I tell the story I want through the things I am creating? The answer to this is a fairly simple one. You let your work be informed by the story you are wanting to tell. This goes some way towards describing the world building that goes into a project or piece of art within this discipline.

I like to split what storytelling is into the five sections below to make it more digestible, so we can cover some of the nuances involved in this process.

Storytelling can be used as a blanket term to cover all of the areas I will cover below. However, breaking this down into the parts below will really help us dig into how important storytelling is at every level of the design process. Plus, there are some subtle differences in how we would approach each area when it comes to design.

THE OVERALL NARRATIVE OF THE STORY

The overall narrative is the term used to describe the story of the thing you are producing. For example, in Shadow of the Colossus by Ico games, the overall narrative is the character's journey to save a princess through the killing of Colossi within the game. So, the narrative would be the story of this journey in its simplest terms.

If we are designing characters, environments, etc., we would just need to know or understand the key elements to inform our designs. So, things like who is the main protagonist, what's the relationship between him and the princess? Even these few details will permeate our design thinking when it comes to designing.

WORLD

World is the overall way you would describe the place the story is set in. So, if Shadow of the Colossus is our example again, the world is a fading fantasy

DOI: 10.1201/9781003500032-9

comparable with medieval times but with magic and giant creatures. The world is relatively empty with sparce life.

Knowing what the world is, is a pivotal scoping tool when it comes to designing anything. All characters and environments are symptomatic of the world they inhabit. Knowing broadly what our world is will act as blinders as we research the subject area. This is really helpful when starting a project. It doesn't mean we will stay within this subject area, but it will give us a useful starting point before we start to evolve our designs.

ENVIRONMENT

The environment is more granular in scale compared to the world view. We are now looking at ruined temples, open fields and glades with rivers within our research process. This is the stuff typically we would be designing and building in a project.

So again, using Shadow of the Colossus as the example (and if you haven't played this game, you really should, it's a masterpiece of storytelling, atmosphere and simplicity), there are ruins that would need to be designed, not just for gameplay purposes but also to embed the story of the world and its past. So, if we were designing these ruins, we would have to dig into what are we trying to communicate? What do we want the space to feel like? Once we know these things, we can start grabbing reference and coming up with ideas for what the spaces could look like.

PLAYER OR VIEWER

The player or viewer is basically us. So, when we think of our reference point of Shadow of the Colossus and storytelling and how this pertains to us, we are asked to take on the control and engagement of the character we are playing. We can pretend we are the character and suspend our disbelief that we are them but there is always going to be a disconnect between us the player and the character. Therefore, it's important that when creating a narrative that we build one for player as well as the character. The motivations for us as the player are very different from that of the character. As the player we need different motivators like engaging world to run around in, meaningful interactions with the characters we encounter. We also need the inputs we make into our controller, mouse and touchscreens to feel right. For both the player and character, there needs to feel like there is progression to the story. This will help both the player and character feel like they are on a journey, which is really important.

CHARACTER

Now, the player and the character are different. This is really important to understand and this can sometimes get muddled up with the player perspective. If we take, for the last time Shadow of the Colossus, we take on the role of Wander the game's protagonist. The character we play also needs motivation like the player themselves. The character needs to be pushed or pulled forward to some form of conclusion and this is done through the story they are involved in. And in Wander's character case, he is trying to save or cure Mono the princess. To do this, the character must kill colossi (spoiler) throughout the world. This then gives the character motivation to move forward, explore and take on the colossi. Along with this, there are some other subtle ways that Wander is motivated to move forward. Things like his horse and sword enable Wander to move through the world in an enjoyable and story-driven way. The horse and objects that Wander uses are brimming with personality and feel right for the world they exist in.

STORYTELLING CONCLUSION

All of the four areas above work together to embed storytelling into every area of the game. This strategy of **World, Environment, Character** and **Player** is also embedded into filmmaking and television, with the **player** being replaced by the viewer in this case.

I see some students not familiar or interested in developing a robust design process, and skip some of these areas, just thinking good design and interesting/engaging story will just happen on its own, leading to underwhelming stories and lacklustre designs as a whole.

When starting out, it is so important to remember that great art always comes out of a robust design and story-driven process.

WORLD BUILDING

Storytelling and the different ways narrative is embedded, as described above all contribute towards the world building of a project. The way I like to imagine, they are two forces both embodying the other, the visual work you produce being a representation of the story that is invisible and underpins it. Both informed by the other. The narrative as it is being constructed in the designer/artist's imagination is visual, but only in the designer/artist's head. We then create this visually, as best we can, as an embodiment of the narrative. Games companies like Fromsoftware, CD Project Red and Naughty Dog are experts at this, and represent the pinnacle of storytelling in this art form.

Chapter 10

Simplifying landscapes

INTRODUCTION TO SIMPLIFYING LANDSCAPES

To get used to the process of designing and building environments and using some of the techniques we have been talking about earlier in the book, it would be a good idea to do a task that helps with this. This task is excellent for those wanting to understand the fundamental thinking process behind environment concept art. The task is really simple to do, and you will get some good work out of it if you practice it regularly.

The task is using visual reference of existing landscapes and breaking it down into two simple values, otherwise known as Notan painting. We will then build upon this and paint some more landscapes using three values.

NOTAN

Notan is the Japanese process of painting with two values, or just in black and using the background (usually white) as the second value.

Ironically, the restrictiveness of this technique is incredibly liberating as a process to use. I first learned of this process at college when I was first learning how to paint. I didn't think much of this process when I first learned of it, but as I moved from a formal learning environment into professional life, I quickly realised how important this technique was and how useful it could be in the design process.

When using this process, it's important to have a plan. What parts of the objects, environment or characters do you want to show and fundamentally what are we creating? When using this process for the first time, try not to be too hard on yourself, this technique can be difficult to get your head around at first, but it's very versatile when mastered. By this it means, just have fun using the process and enjoy its simplicity, both in application and results.

DOI: 10.1201/9781003500032-10

Notan at its heart is creating readable silhouettes and shapes. This is primarily because Notan is a simple binary choice. Is it black or white? Because of the simplicity in this technique, it does mean that how you organise the shapes and form is your main concern, which takes the pressure off detailing. Detailing is only achievable through the edges of the shapes you create, as well as the organisation of the space these shapes occupy. It is possible to get a tonne of detail using this technique, but for the exercises we will be doing we will try and keep it simple, and just establish the initial read.

Task: Notan environments

We are now going to paint a series of Notan environments using visual reference.

- Choose six environment reference pictures.
- Choose pictures with high contrast.
- Paint out the pictures with just one brush and a dark grey tone.
- Focus mainly on the overall shapes first then scale brush down for medium and small shapes.
- Use a big brush to cover large areas.
- Take around 20 minutes per painting.

Photos to do studies from.

First, grab a selection of images. Higher contrast images are easier to work with if this is your first time doing them.

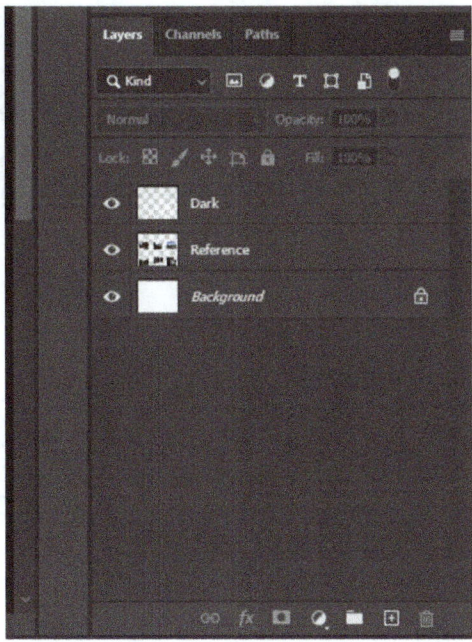

Layers panel.

After I have all my images present, I merge the layers down to one reference layer. You can do this by right clicking on the top layer you want to merge.

Boxes for the pictures.

Create boxes the approximate size of the reference images to work in.

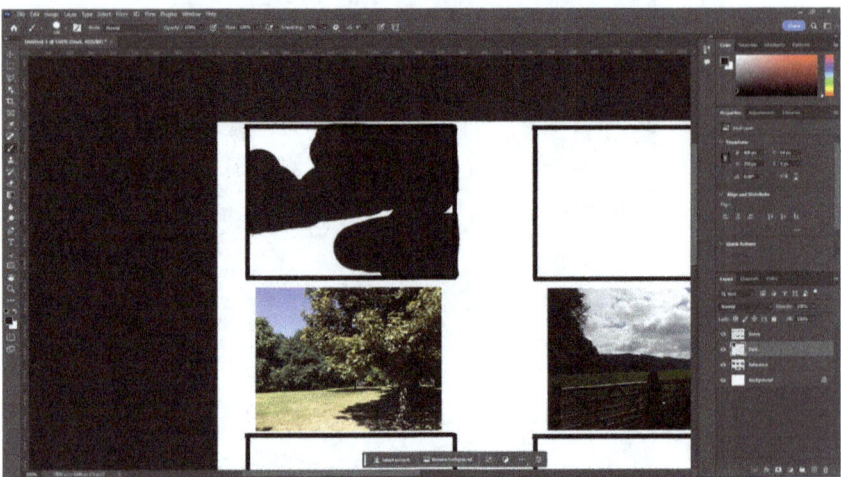

Initial blockout.

Block in the rough shape of the masses you want to create. We will come back to these once all the initial passes are completed.

Two initial blockouts.

I tend to spend around 5–10 minutes on each one, depending on the complexity of the image. It can be hard to decide where to paint but just go with your gut.

All blockouts.

All of the initial blocking out is done. Some of the big shapes might need repainting because they are in the wrong position. And now we move onto the detailing part.

Refining of the blockout.

I work through the initial paintings above and now go in and add more detail. Take as long as you need for this part but taking around 10–15 minutes for each one is the optimal amount of time you should spend. Any more than this and it's diminishing returns.

All refined.

The final stage is doing a final pass with a smaller brush and adding more detail to the external shape.

Snow and lake.

It's up to you to decide when to stop and leave the image. I spent about an extra five minutes on the rightmost image, but both are readable and convey what I needed.

Tip: If you are struggling to see or define the light or dark areas squint, this can help simplify the image and stop you looking at the details.

It's important to keep practicing the Notan way of painting. This will really help you understand the fundamentals of visual language. I see the greatest level of improvement in the shortest amount of time from my students when this exercise is practiced on a regular basis.

PAINTING SIMPLE SHAPES IN THREE VALUES

Now that we have used the Notan technique to paint out simple environments, we can now add to the complexity of this technique by adding another value. When adding another value to your workflow, it's important to not forget the lessons learned from the Notan tasks. What I mean by this is, when laying in your values, make sure you concentrate on the shape of the object and getting it accurate. I have seen people really struggle when adding a third value. Mainly because they struggle with where to use this extra value. How to address this is by structuring how we lay in our first two values.

The first task is assessing the image you are using as reference and wanting to paint. Decide where you want the lightest and darkest values to be. Similar to the way you did with Notan paintings. Now, this is the tricky bit. What information do you still need to communicate to the viewer? And there are lots of different answers to this, none of them wrong. And all specific to the person painting the image. So, let's go through the main ways of using the third value and how I tackle it depending on the image I am using as reference below.

CLASSIC LANDSCAPE

What I call a classic landscape is a clear foreground, midground and background, containing no clear focal points. The image below shows this with open fields, trees and sky. With the clear value splits being the trees representing the dark values, midtones representing the fields and grass areas and sky being the light values. You could rearrange these values and play around with how light or dark they are to create a different feeling image altogether. There are degrees of right and wrong here, so just play around and see what happens. Don't be scared of getting it "wrong". You will learn far more from trying things out.

View from the train.

Looking at the reference photo I judge where the three values we are going to use will be placed. This will be slightly different for every image.

Getting started with the view.

First, I have laid in a simple light grey value for the sky. This is the first value.

 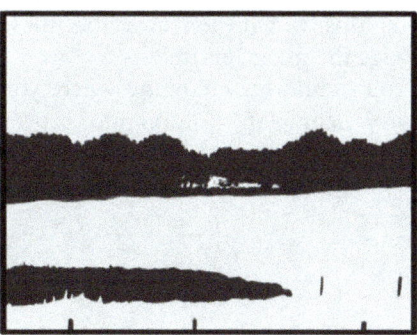

Blocking out the view.

Next, I put down the darkest value to represent the trees, bushes and other dark areas in the image. This is our second value.

Refinement of the view.

Finally, we lay down our midtones, which represent the fields in the fore- and midground. This is our final value.

AREA OF INTEREST IN THE LANDSCAPE

What I would call an area of interest landscape, is a landscape that has some clear focal points that you are intending the viewer to look at. This could be anything that sticks out from the landscape. It could be a strikingly different tree or body of water, or a building/ruin, like in the image below.

When using three values like on the image below, we use the lightest value for the sky and the darkest value for pretty much everything else. We then use our midtones for detailing the focal point (castle). We could use our midtones to paint some other details in the environment instead of the castle but by doing this we tell the viewer that these areas are important. This would then change the image entirely.

You should try changing where you put values if you are unsure or don't have a clear plan. You might discover some happy accidents in the process. Again, don't be scared just have fun painting.

Craster castle.

Again, we look at the reference and judge where the three values will go.

 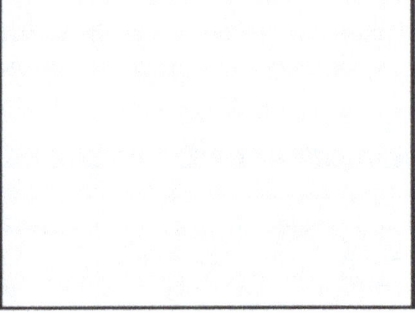

A frame for craster.

Like before we lay in our lightest value, which is the sky in this case. This represents our first value.

Craster blockout.

We then lay in our darkest value of the castle and foreground hill. This is our second value.

Craster in three values.

Finally, we use our mid grey value to show detail within the focal point of our image, this being the castle. This is our third value.

Task: Simple value environments

We are now going to paint a series of value environments, using visual reference.

- Choose foure environment reference pictures.
- Choose pictures with high contrast.
- Paint out the pictures with just one brush.
- Start with the sky usually a light value.
- Next the land in either a dark or mid value.
- Finally, the last value to add detail or area(s) of interest.
- Focus mainly on the overall shapes first, then scale brush down for medium and small shapes.
- Use a big brush to cover large areas.
- Take around 20–30 minutes per painting.

Waterfall.

I create a box the approximate size of the reference you are using and then I block out the sky in a light grey value.

Waterfall blockout.

I then block out the side rocks and foliage, so I can get a sense of detail and framing of the waterfall.

Waterfall shape.

On a separate layer behind the rocks and foliage, I add another dark layer to be the rocks behind the waterfall.

  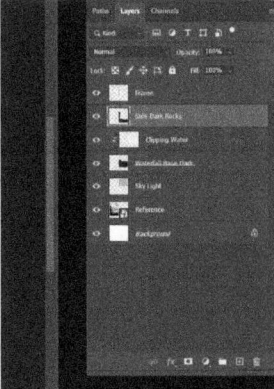

Waterfall layers.

I then add a clipping mask to the dark layer we have just painted and paint a very light grey to represent the waterfall itself.

Waterfall finished.

Finally, I define the rocks and foliage a bit more at the sides and then use a brush with texture to erase out of the white waterfall to reveal the dark rocks behind.

TAKING PICTURES

So far, we have found and painted environments and landscapes. The next step is going to be finding and taking pictures and compositions. This will get you thinking about the way an image is structured and what the world looks like through a different lens.

This process of going and taking pictures is a really useful one, because it helps imbed good compositional awareness, which will improve your eye. Going out with your camera and really looking at the world around you has a number of benefits. The main one of these being your senses. Many think that your eyes and hands do all the work in both taking pictures and also making art. However, in the same way that using a reference picture you found on the internet to paint, or draw is useful. It is even more useful to stand in the place you are intending to draw or paint. The way you experience the sounds and smells, as well as the sights has hidden benefits to art making. Standing in the place gives the artist context and a deeper level of understanding and appreciation for what makes a compelling scene. Drawing from nature is a great way to use all your senses.

Environment moodboard.

Taking pictures when something catches your eye could lead to some interesting painting.

Even if you just go out and take pictures to use as painting and drawing reference later, you will still get some residual benefit of actually having stood in the space. All the things you saw, smelt and heard will still be in your memory, just slightly more diluted than physically painting in that spot. You also won't have the added paranoia of someone watching over your shoulder and asking questions, which you would get from painting in the space. I work like this quite a bit and I find it the most enjoyable way to work.

Task: Take some pictures

You are now going to go outside and take some pictures of anything that grabs your interest.

- Head to somewhere that is enjoyable and feels safe.
- Keep your phone or camera ready to take pictures.
- Take as many pictures as you like with interesting compositions.
- Don't overthink it.
- Keep moving and shooting.
- Use all your senses, listen, smell and see.
- When home look at the pictures, try to see the values.

COMPOSITION 1—Understanding Shapes (youtube.com) (https://www.youtube.com/watch?v=wg-So3ElA8g)

MASTERS STUDIES

Master's studies are another good way of honing your skills as an artist/designer. This is the process of looking at a masters painting, drawing or illustration and re-drawing/painting it. The purpose of this is to understand not just the painting, but also the techniques/decisions made by the artist. Absorbing some of this good practice through the act of recreation.

Master's studies can range in subject matter as well as style. There are landscapes, scenes or portraits as main categories to look at and study from. The aim is to select works that help you understand one of the fundamentals, like value, anatomy, composition, etc.

One of the reasons we use master painter/illustrator to study from is because of their understanding of the fundamentals. It's really important that you study from the best if you want your process to improve.

When producing studies of master's paintings, you would typically take one of these paintings and produce a simplified version of it, using three or so values.

Focusing on how they structure their painting in terms of shape and value.

Task: Masters studies

Find some masters paintings or illustrations that you find interesting. I have included a list of good artists and illustrators to look at below. You will then paint or draw these using simple values.

- Choose five works you want to study.
- Start by pinpointing the values first and boiling them down to three at most.
- Spend time nailing down the shape of the objects in the scene.
- Work with a big brush initially and scale down to add shape detail.
- Work with confidence and don't worry about the end result.
- Take 20–30 minutes per study.

LIST OF MASTER PAINTERS AND ILLUSTRATORS

Below is a list of master painters and illustrators that are worth a look. When looking through these artists and their work, try to pick works that you are able to break down and are able to see where you could place the values.

Mead Schaeffer
Norman Rockwell
N.C. Wyeth
J.C. Leyendecker
Howard Pyle

Dean Cornwell
Bob Peak
Caspar David Friedrich
J.M.W. Turner
Alfred de Breanski
Andreas Achenbach
Ivan Shishkin
Albert Bierstadt
Johan Christian Dahl
Isaac Levitan
John Burton
Jeremy Mann
Richard Schmid

Masters paintings.

For exercises like this I try to focus on the big shapes first, once this is established, I move onto the medium and smaller shapes.

https://www.youtube.com/watch?v=AGFs6EaHlDI

CINEMA STUDIES

When trying to learn how to compose a believable image, there are a number of exercises you can do to begin to understand this complicated process. One excellent way to begin to build an understanding of composition and storytelling within an image is through looking at cinema stills. The beauty of looking at something like a cinema still is that these scenes and stills have been curated and agonised over by concept artists, directors and cinematographers, throughout the production of making the film. So, there is a level of quality associated with these stills. So, when drawing or painting from them you are learning parts of what was going on in the head of the people involved in production.

Painting stills from cinema or TV is a really good way to understand storytelling and composition. The really good directors spend many months planning shots to elicit a specific emotion from the viewer. All of this good practice will transfer into your own work when doing these types of exercises on a regular basis.

There are a number of excellent directors, with captivating visual styles that are great to study. I have included a list of these below, but feel free to work from directors of films that you like and feel passionate about.

Stanley Kubrick
David Lean
David Fincher
Alfred Hitchcock
Akira Kurosowa
Ridley Scott
Nocolas Winding Refn
Jane Campion
Quentin Tarantino
Davis Lynch

Task: Cinema stills

Cinema studies follow the same principle as the master's studies in terms of the processes used. You will then paint or draw these using simple values.

- Choose six stills you want to study.
- Start by pinpointing the values first and boiling them down to three at most.
- Spend time nailing down the shape of the objects in the scene.
- Work with a big brush initially and scale down to add shape detail.
- Work with confidence and don't worry about the end result.
- Take 20–30 minutes per study.

There are a number of websites to find stills from, but the one below in my opinion is the best to use.
https://www.evanerichards.com/

Tip: Try and pick high contrast images to start with, to make seeing the values and shapes easier.

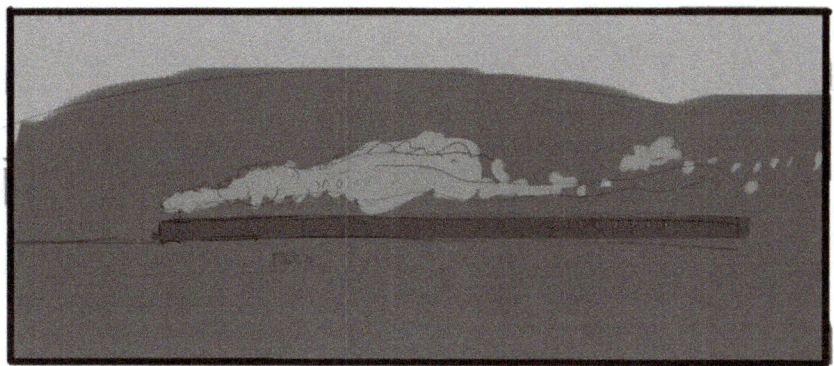

Hogwarts and Dunkirk.

Breaking complex stills into three simple manageable values is the key in these exercises.

Task: Cinema stills the sequel

We have tackled cinema stills as an exercise, we can now focus on a little bit more detail and consistency. How we are going to do this is through more enhanced cinema studies.

- Choose three stills you want to study from the same film.
- Start by pinpointing the values first and boiling them down to four at most.
- Spend time nailing down the shape of the objects in the scene.

- Work with a big brush initially and scale down to add shape detail.
- Work with confidence and don't worry about the end result.
- Take 25–35 minutes per study.

For this task, I choose two stills from my favourite movie "2001: A Space Odyssey", by Stanley Kubrick. I chose this film because of its exceptional design and shot framing. And I chose these specific stills because of their visual contrast.

As we have discussed before, I first analyse the still and try to work out roughly where my values will sit. Whenever possible I try to lay in the background that all the other shapes sit on. And if we use the images below, look at how much of the still is background. For the topmost image about half of the still is background. And for the bottom one it's probably around 80%. Think about this for a second. With one value and sweep of a brush, we can complete over half of the image.

2001 blockout.

I start by seeing where the values will be placed and blocking out the simple statement for each still.

2001 refined.

I then refine the simple statement and carve out the shapes of the objects in the scene.

2001 three values.

Now I add my third value and figure out what are the things I want to define in the painting.

2001 finished.

I use the final fourth value to add detail to the most important parts of the images, the apes and pod.

Practicing capturing a scene with limited values is the fastest way to level up the core fundamentals that you will use. Adding the fourth value, as shown above is a luxury when using limited values and I only use this on areas that I think the viewer might need more information on. By using this value in limited places, you create contrast. The contrast being detail vs no detail, which draws the viewers eye where you want it to look. Practice these techniques and you will be surprised how little detail you need to build a highly detailed meaningful image.

Chapter 11

3D

3D MODELLING AND ENVIRONMENT CONCEPT ART

As well as having drawing and painting in 2D as a tool for making environment concept art, we also have 3D tools at our disposal. All of the fundamentals that we have discussed so far still apply to 3D tools, and how we would use them for creating designs and art works.

Now, let us first talk about what we mean by 3D modelling. 3D modelling is used to describe building an object, character or environment in three dimensions. And just like with the drawing and painting process, you start with the large shapes first and then move onto the medium and small shapes after this. We use the big shapes as an anchor for the medium and small shapes. The only real difference is that you are building things in three dimensions, rather than two.

USING SIMPLE PRIMITIVES

3D modelling, using primitives, whiteboxing or greyboxing are all terms used to describe the process of building within a 3D package. For us as concept artists, this mainly means using very simple cubes, cones, cylinders, etc. This technique is used in lots of different areas of game development but is primarily used by concept artists to block out simple scenes and experiment with composition. Once you have a very simple scene or composition, you would then use this as a base. You would then take a screenshot of the image from a few different angles and paint over it in a digital painting package, like Photoshop or Procreate. This didn't used to be the case, it's only fairly recently that concept artists have used this technique as part of their normal everyday pipeline.

I tend to use 3D as a technique only when confronted with really complex scenes or environments, or when the perspective of a scene is posing problems. For example, interiors with lots of objects and furniture is a situation where I would use 3D first (again, only with simple primitives). Another situation where I might use 3D to solve problem, if I am designing a fairly complex building or collection of buildings that need to be accurate. Using 3D in the cases above can solve perspective and lighting problems before I even commit to a sketch or painting.

Another major benefit in using 3D is compositions and angle variety. What I mean by this is, once I use simple primitives and low level 3D blockouts to solve a 3D problem, you then have the option to rotate, zoom and find other compositions in the model you have just made, to find other interesting shots. This can be a strong incentive to use 3D as a base to get most artists started. However, you would have to weigh this against, the time it would take to block out a scene and then paint over against just painting it without the use of 3D. A really good artist to look at for this is Jose Vega (https://www. youtube.com/artofjosevega) who has quite a few videos on how to use this technique.

DRAWBACKS OF 3D

Like every technique and piece of software, 3D can solve certain problems and cause others. I have explained what specific instances I would choose 3D as a starter option when creating environmental concept art. However, it can have its drawbacks, so it's important to see how it can best work for you.

Here are some drawbacks when using 3D for environmental concept art:

- **Barrier to entry:** It can put some people off having to learn 3D. It is a whole new workflow and pipeline to add to the other things you still need to work on.
- It can be difficult to get your head around the new user interface of 3D software, as well as how this translates to creating a final design idea.
- **It feels wrong:** I have heard this quite a few times regarding the feel of using 3D to create traditionally 2D images. There is a massive amount of muscle memory that we have.

Task: Build a basic 3D exterior diorama

For this next task, we are going to dig into building a simple 3D environment diorama in the 3D programme of your choice. I will be using Blender for this, because it's free, relatively easy to use and I have used it before for this type of task. Once we have built the 3D space, we are going to use it as a basis for creating compositions and paint overs.

- Gather reference of the 3D space you are going to build.
- Spend time nailing down the shape of the objects in the scene.
- Keep the block out simple.
- Just resize objects and don't do detailed modelling.

- Take 40–60 minutes to block out the simple scene but take as long as you need if this seems unfamiliar.

Here is a link to a good reference moodboard for what we are going to build.
https://uk.pinterest.com/lees0301/snowy-cabin/

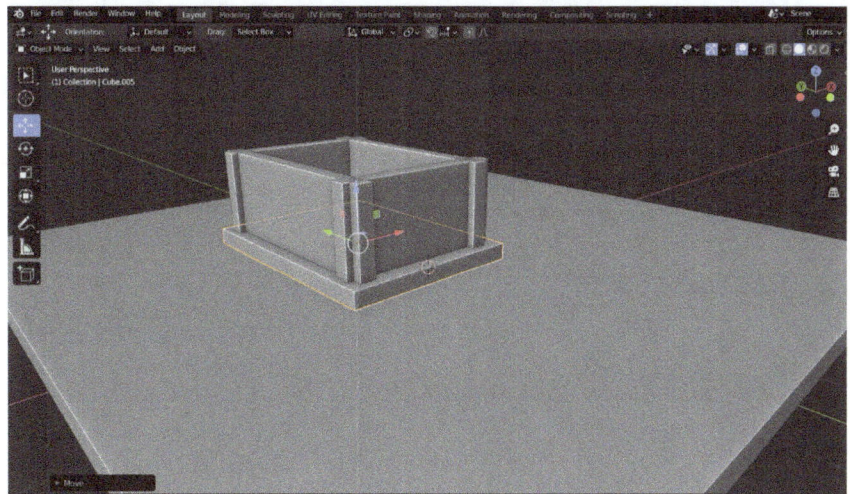

Four walls and a floor.

I try to get the big shapes done first, ground, floor and walls. Just to get an idea of shape and the basic forms of the cabin.

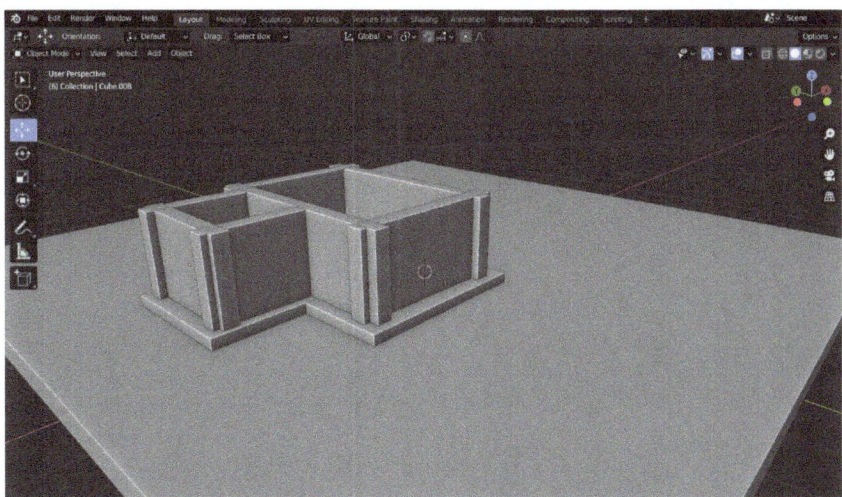

More walls and a floor.

I then add another side room based on references I have gathered to make the scene more interesting.

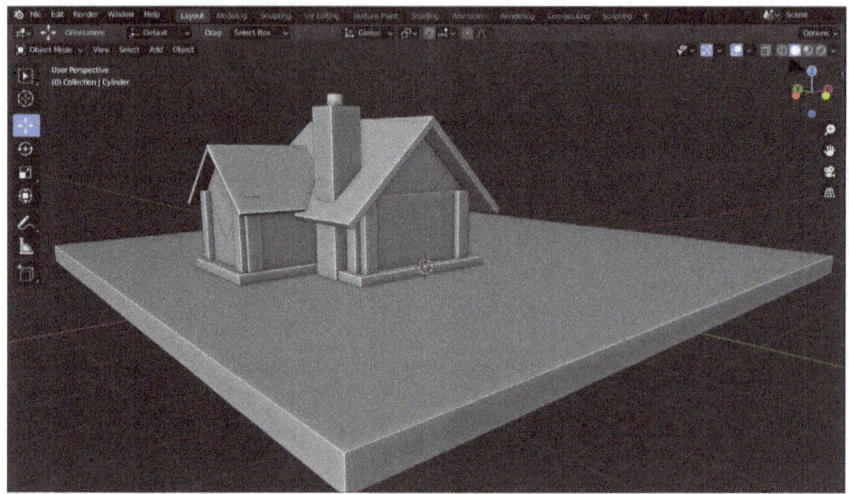

3D cabin.

I then add the roof and chimney. At this stage the cabin is readable, and this would be ok to leave it here and begin painting if you wanted to.

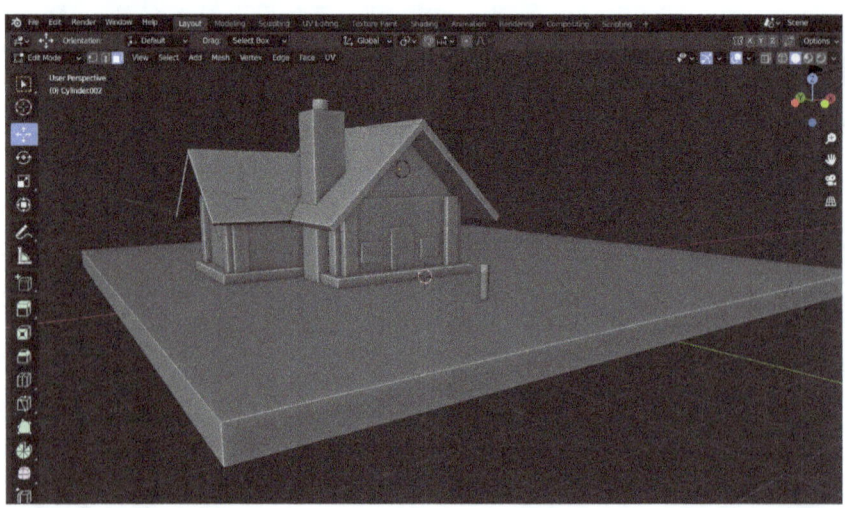

A human for scale.

I add a couple of interesting details to the house to establish windows and doors and a character for size reference. This is where I would usually stop.

Cabin with a fence.

If you wanted to, you could add even more detail but I wouldn't personally. All this can be added through sketching over the top. And it can often be distracting with too much detail.

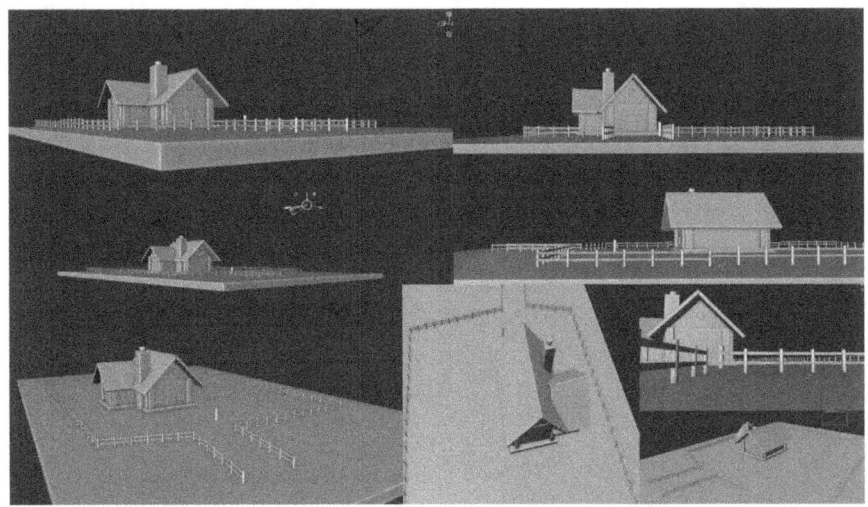

3D composition moodboard.

Working in 3D is a great way to establish compositions. One 3D model can offer many compositional options.

Once you have built the rough block out, you can then use this to paint over. Adding lots more detail can be useful for some people at the 3D phase. But I find it harder to be spontaneous when adding details and design ideas, with a very detailed design underneath.

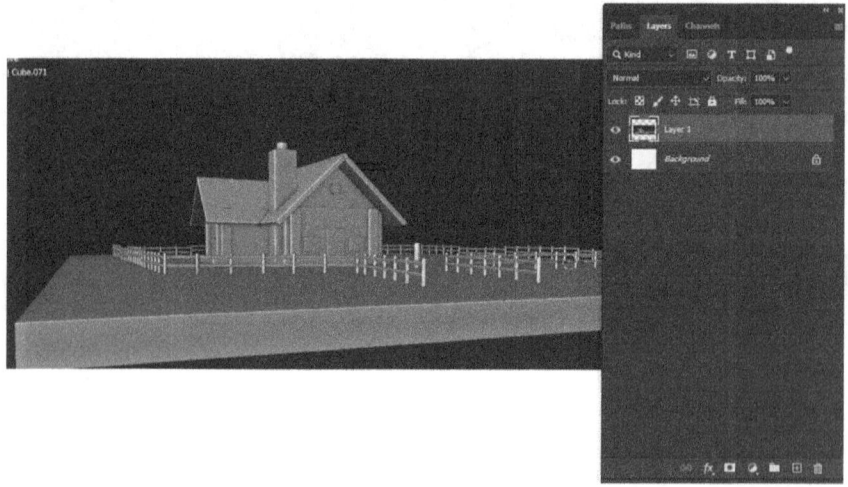

Final cabin composition.

Having taken the 3D image into Photoshop I lower the opacity to about 40% and change the layer from normal to multiply, so I can see the blockout below whilst painting my values.

Desaturated final composition.

With the image now lighter it isn't competing for my attention when painting.

Light value on the 3D paintover.

I work with four values in mind initially, with the sky being a light value. I put this in first because it gives me a good base to work from on the rest of the painting.

Dark value for cabin and fields.

I now add the darkest value in which is the cabin and the grounds around it. I block it all in as one to start with and even extend the canvas to add more of the background into the shot.

Introducing a third value for detail.

I then paint in the fence on the same dark value layer to tie the background and the foreground together. I don't stick rigidly to the 3D model at this stage, I find it more important to paint freely and letting stuff happen.

Final cabin in the woods.

At this point I look at reference material to see if there is anything I can add to the scene to make it more interesting. I add trees to the background and define the fence posts in the midground. I also start the process of picking out parts of the cabin that I need to read like verticals and windows.

Task: Building a simple concept environment space

For this next task you will be building a very simple 3D concept environment space, using the 3D software of your choice. Start by defining what it is that you are going to build. Not just physically what the space is but also its purpose and tone.

Designing something that doesn't exist and trying to tell a story in your scene can be confusing and difficult at times. The best way to solve some of these problems is by choosing a subject that you feel passionate about or familiar with.

- Find a page of reference material to start you off.
- Add more reference if you are confused.
- Keep it simple and don't over model the scene.
- Use simple shapes and no detailed modelling.
- Remember this needs to be understandable at a glance and is going to be painted over.
- Keep rotating the camera to check interesting compositions.
- Take 60 minutes or as long as you need to model the scene.

Cathedral moodboard.

A good moodboard is always the best starting place when designing or building a space. Above is an example of one I am using to build my cathedral space.

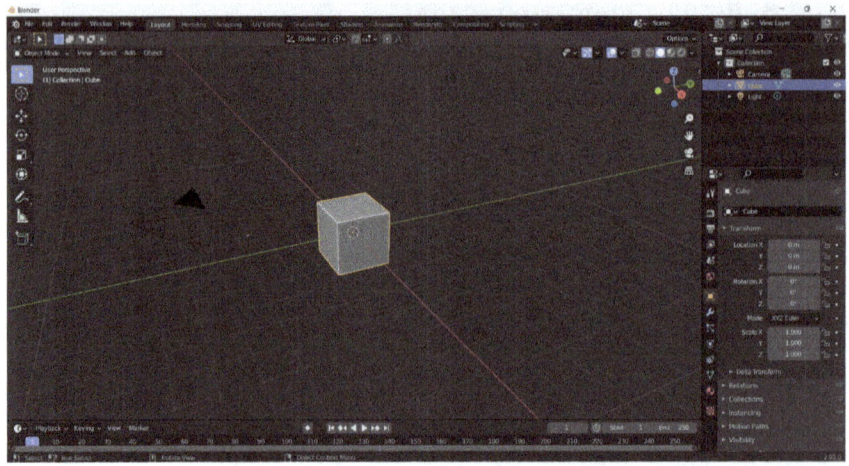

3D cube.

Once you open Blender, start by selecting General from the options. I delete the standard cube presented here with the delete key on your keyboard.

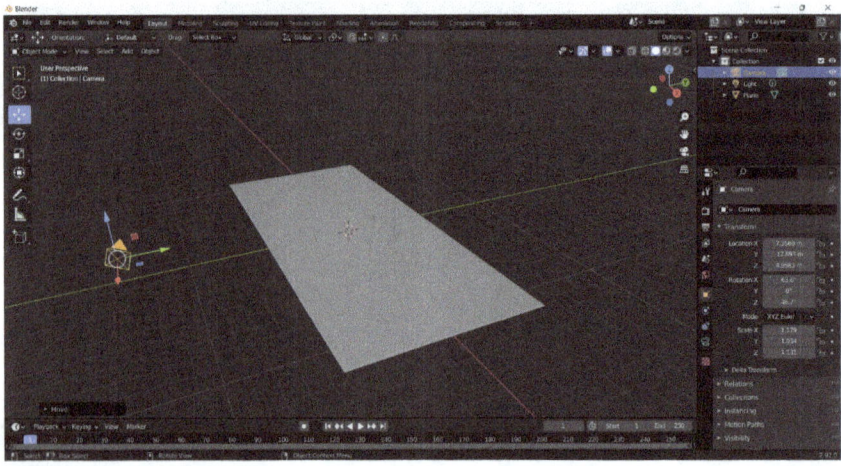

3D plane.

Add a plane from the "add" drop down menu at the top of the screen. The plane represents the ground and interior space within the cathedral environment.

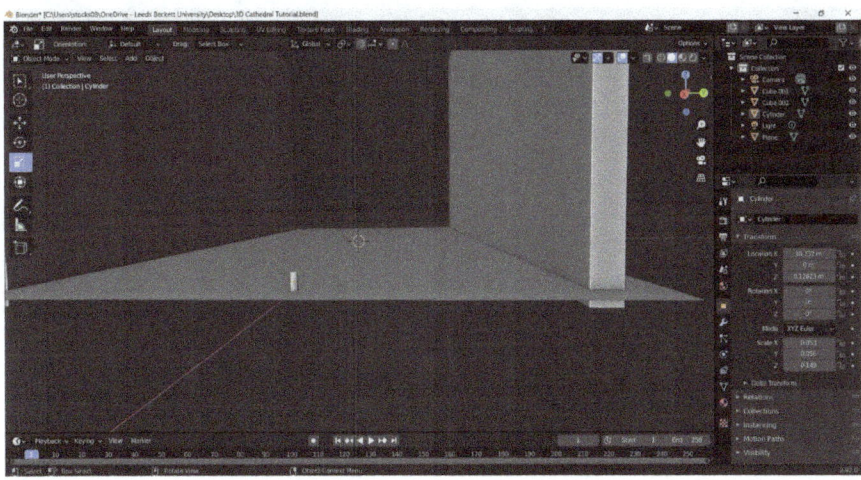

Scale.

Once I have a rough idea of size for the floor plane, I add a wall and a small cylinder to represent a character. This is essential for establishing size.

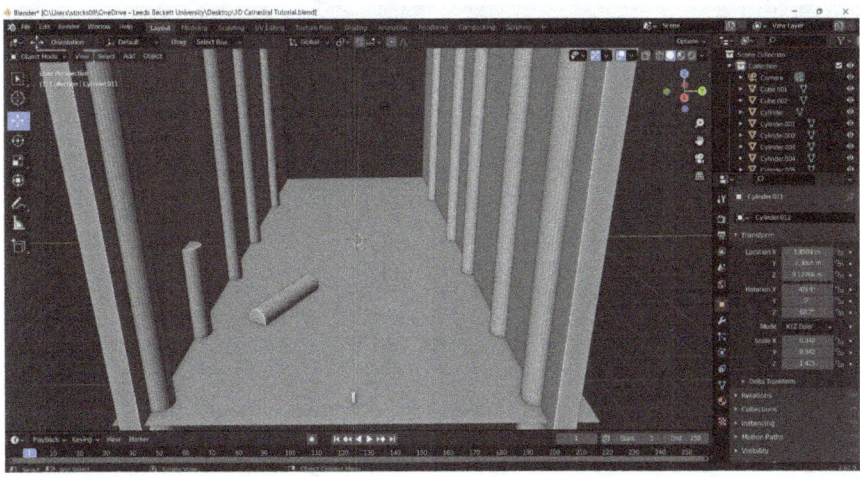

Pillars.

I then add pillars to the scene. I start with one, get the size and shape right, then I duplicate and place.

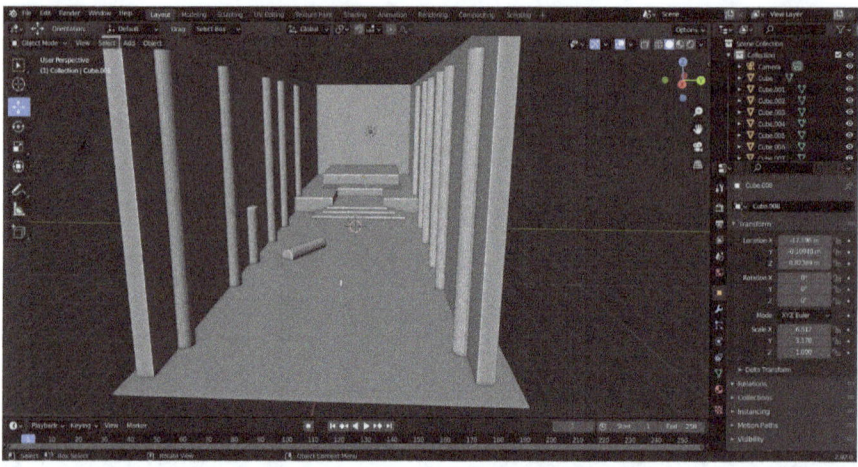

Throne area.

I added in an uplifted back section where the focal point will be in the environment. These are just simple cubes that have been scaled to the appropriate sizes.

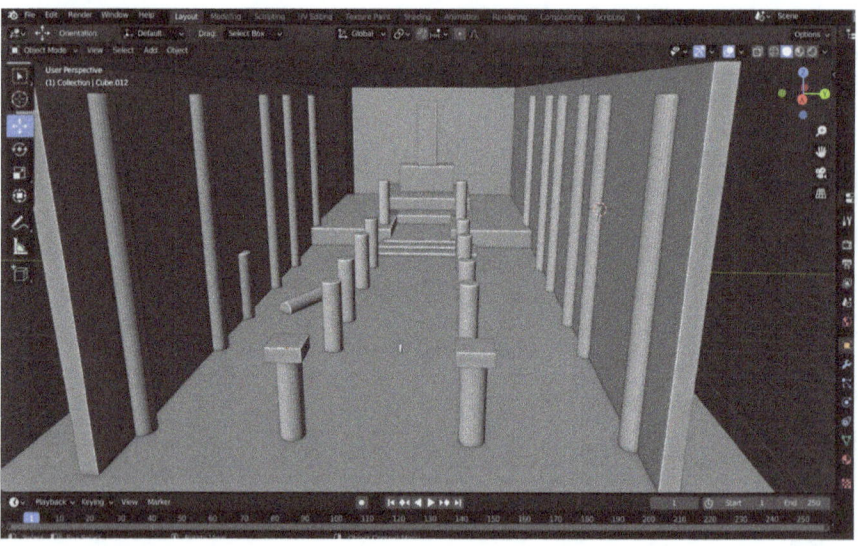

More pillars.

I now add plinths where statues will stand in the space.

Final composition. Final composition viewport shader.

I have added beams on the roof, primitive statues and rough boarded up windows at the back of the room. This is also the composition we will be using for the paint over process. The rightmost image is the viewport shader image within Blender, with the light mover around to the best angle.

Notan blockout.

It's worth mentioning at this stage that I always try and think about the space that I create being either a game space or a set for a film/television show. What angles will I show? Where would the player be walking, etc. These simple thoughts will keep your designs on track, for the most part as you design.

Final detailed Notan.

Chapter 12

Environment concept artists

There are lots of great environment concept artists, working across games, film and television. We are really lucky to have so many concept artists providing video content on sites like YouTube and Twitch, showing you how to build works. I have included a list below of some of the best YouTube links to some of these artists:

Victor Stairs: https://www.youtube.com/channel/UCkMK-WJFcixvnKVJcx_9DQQ/videos

Jose Vega: https://www.youtube.com/channel/UClzf76f0GGhrQ_tPSVRcGsg

Jordan Grimmer: https://www.youtube.com/@JordanGrimmer

Grady Frederick: https://www.youtube.com/@gradyfrederickart

ArtTrain Academy: https://www.youtube.com/@arttrainacademy6626/videos

James Paick: https://www.youtube.com/@jamespaickART

FZD: https://www.youtube.com/@FZDSCHOOL

All of the artists and video pages above are great resources for any level and offer an amazing insight into both the quality of work you should be aiming to produce and useful tips to make that a reality.

ENVIRONMENT CONCEPT ART PROCESS

Creating 2D environment concept art begins with a strong foundation in visual storytelling and composition. The process typically starts with research and gathering references to understand the setting's mood, architecture, lighting and cultural context. Whether it's a futuristic cityscape, a mystical forest or a post-apocalyptic ruin, you need a clear narrative or theme to inform the visual choices you make. Begin by sketching or painting thumbnail compositions that explore different compositions, focal points and spatial relationships. These rough drawings/paintings are crucial for testing layout ideas quickly and without the pressure of detail.

Once a compelling composition is selected, move into more detailed line work and value studies to define form and lighting. Consider, weather and

DOI: 10.1201/9781003500032-12

overall atmosphere to guide your lighting decisions and colour palette. Use overlap techniques through digital painting to build depth, starting with background elements and moving towards the foreground. Focus on creating a sense of scale through overlap, relative size and range of value. The key is to guide the viewer's eye naturally through the scene while reinforcing the mood and story. Iteration is essential then refine, adjust and get feedback to ensure the environment feels immersive and coherent.

The fundamental process of creating environment concept art will now put to the test in our last environment task below.

ENVIRONMENT CONCEPT ART CHANGING SMALL DETAILS

Designing a concept environment from scratch with or without a design brief to guide you can be incredibly daunting and confusing for beginner artists. One really good way to begin the process of designing a concept environment is through using real environments to guide the design process. Using images like the ones below can scaffold the process and give you a blueprint to build off of. What I would do in conjunction with this is get into the habit of changing small details in the space, using other picture(s). Slowly using multiple images and evolving them slowly when painting is an excellent way of building confidence and competence in your workflow, and we will look at how to do this in the next task.

Task: Study to environment concept art

Choose any two environment pictures that have a similar composition, ideally one with a distinct structure we can change.

- Assess the image you are painting and what you want to change.
- Establish the composition with 3–4 simple values.
- Don't focus on detail, just the big shapes.
- Take about 40–50 minutes to paint out the scene.
- Choose the thing you are changing and erase the original structure and replace it in the same value.

This task is a really good way of mimicking most of the techniques you will use while creating environment concept art. Being able to evolve and adapt your visual library and the research used into other interesting compositions is an important tool to have in your toolbox. Once you are confident with your fundamental skills I would suggest practicing this task repeatedly.

Bright ruins. Church grounds.

The two images above are the ones we will be using to adapt in the next task. Feel free to use your own images or there is a link to my Pinterest boards. Try to choose images that you can imagine changing and start small. It might be changing the shape of a tree or rock.

https://uk.pinterest.com/lees0301/

Blank frame.

I start with a rough frame and think about where I am going to place my values. Of course, this can all change as we start to lay the values in.

Grey sky.

I try to start with a value that I am really sure about and in this case, I know that the sky is the lightest area and will provide great contrast for the darker elements overlapping it.

Ruins shape.

I now focus my attention to the most important part of the process, blocking in the shapes and making sure they are readable. You should take your time with this part and make sure all the elements are in the right place and show a good amount of external detail on the silhouette.

Detailing third value.

Now I lay in my final mid value tone to describe the internal detail of the environment. I work within the shape I have already defined and simply add the lighter grey value and erase the grey value as needed to reveal the black value underneath. At this point I would consider the painting done (within the confines of the task) and move onto changing the elements within.

Church change.

Chapter 13

Ideas

IDEAS AND WHERE THEY COME FROM

Ideas are an essential commodity for a concept artist. Ideas are the currency that we deal in, so the more we have of these the better the chance of success. The more ideas we generate the better we get at understanding which ones will work and which ones won't.

One of the scariest things for any designer is generating cool ideas that resonate with the player or viewer. All early stage designers get the fear from time to time. Fortunately, ideas come from our past and also from the world around us. This means we potentially have an endless supply of them at our very fingertips, if we look.

THE FEAR

All artists at some point will get the fear. The fear can be many different things related to both your art and the process of making it. The fear is something that most artists feel at some point in their career and can be debilitating and very stressful. The fear can manifest itself in a number of ways, many of which I have personally experienced and had to work through or overcome.

Fear of your work not being at the standard you want

This is probably the most common one and most associated with artists who are starting out on their creative journey. Looking at the work of concept artists online both inspires people to become concept artists and can also deter people because of the standard of the work. This is sometimes exacerbated because getting to that level or standard seems impenetrable. One thing that people try to do to solve this problem is by focusing on the detail of the work they try to produce. Detail in this case refers to the internal rendering of the thing you are designing. And this is totally understandable, given this is often perceived as the thing that drew you to the piece of work or art in the first place. However, this is the opposite of what you should be doing as a beginner.

DOI: 10.1201/9781003500032-13

The internal detail in the grand scheme of things and most importantly from a development perspective, is the least important thing to concentrate on.

Fear of not being able to come up with ideas

This is another fear most commonly associated with new artists. When starting out I thought ideas were a finite resource, and once you use up all your good ideas, you were done. Thankfully, this isn't the case when infact ideas are endless. In the same way your body needs food to survive and a balance of healthy food for your body to thrive. Your mind needs nourishment. This nourishment comes in the form of being curious about the world around you. Looking at things that inspire you, other concept art works, paintings, art, or TV, games or movies. All of this contributes to mind nourishment and the continuous generation of ideas. A really good way to speed up this nourishment is to get outside of your comfort zone and engage with things that you normally wouldn't. If you love sci-fi movies, try a period drama instead.

The works that you love, in games, films and television shows, at some point will have gone through a rigorous design process, and this is the primary reason we gravitate towards them as consumers. This includes everything from the characters, world and things in it. Even the words they say and actions they do. All of these things will have gone through a rigorous iterative design process. They will have been inspired by real moments in someone's life, a film someone has seen, a character in a game and a million other things.

We have to adopt the same principles when we design anything, especially when starting out.

Chapter 14

Character concept art

CHARACTER CONCEPT ART INTRODUCTION

The process you should be using for designing and developing excellent characters is very similar to the process we have already talked about for environment concept art.

Developing interesting characters is all about storytelling first and foremost.

How do I tell a story with a character design? The answer is right under our noses. We see character design every day, in the shops we visit, on the streets we walk and in the places we pass through. Every person we see in every day of our lives is a walking, talking, sitting, story, and the best type of stories are real ones.

And the first part of how to begin this process is rooted in research.

The process for designing characters falls into three processes:

- Research
- Iteration
- Final designs

These three areas are the fundamental building blocks from which artworks are made.

It's important to remember that these stages of development work very similar to what we covered in the environment concept art section of this book.

Research comes first and consists of multiple stages. First, it's a good idea to have a broad idea as to who or what the character is. Think about what world or environment they belong to. We are all symptomatic of our environment and surroundings, you should remember this whilst you design your characters.

The next step is establishing tonally what the world feels like and where the character sits within it? I would usually do this through my moodboards or visual reference. This will act as the anchor to your work in terms of the tone of the character.

The next step is grabbing practical reference in the form of things you would see on the character.

DOI: 10.1201/9781003500032-14

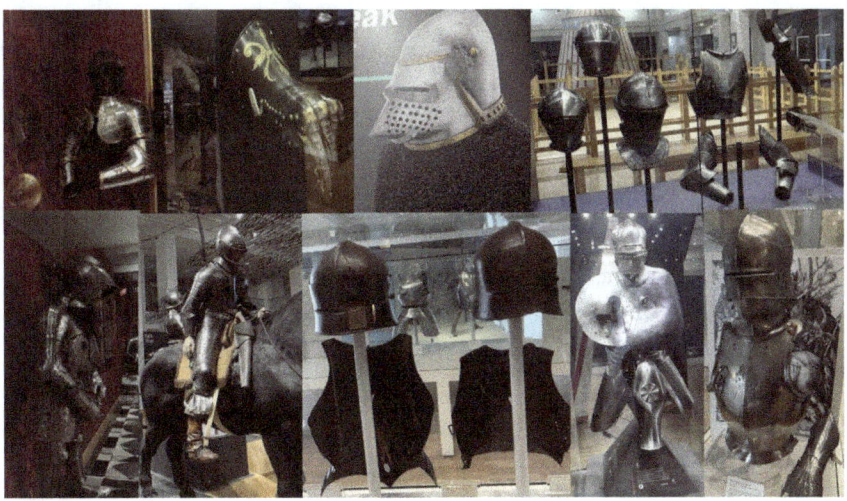

Knight moodboard.

After we have reference, we would typically then begin the design process through iteration. Iteration can be either through sketches or paintings and this is down to the personal preference of the artist doing the work. We would try and produce ideas and designs with just enough detail to convey the design. We would then move onto the next idea and continue this cycle until we are happy with some of the designs.

After we have design options in the form of iterations, we then take one and start to really define its shape and detail. This could be through adding values or starting to add colour/texture to the designs. At this point we have our character design.

Again, this is a simplified version of the pipeline of a character concept artist.

CHARACTER SHAPE

Shape is the most important part of designing a character, as it is with environment. It is the structure that tells the person looking at it what or who the character is. The more detailed the silhouette of the character, the more information and nuance you are communicating to the viewer. As stated earlier in the book, sometimes you need to produce detailed silhouettes, for example, if you have a variety of complete designs. And sometimes you will be wanting to produce looser designs, without getting into a high level of detailed finish. The example for this would be if you are right at the start of the design process and just generating character design ideas. These designs would be exploratory sketches and paintings and will be completed fairly quickly, usually 10–20 minutes sketches. This is just to get the ideas out onto the canvas, these ideas are just that and would still need to go through a process of design and iteration. As the design becomes more realised, so do the iterations and the silhouettes. All of these processes and the work you produce are nothing without shape. Without shape we don't have a character.

Everybody at some point has looked at a piece of character concept art and thought, how the hell have they designed and painted this? The simple answer is through the fundamentals the artist has used. The most important of these and the one to start with is shape.

ANATOMY

Anatomy is the term used to describe the body structure of living things. For our purposes, anatomy represents what the human body looks like, what shape it makes, and how it can be used to tell stories.

Although it can be advantageous to understand how the human body works, it is more important that you can see and simplify the shape of the human body down and represent it to communicate the things you need it to. The human body is the most complex thing on the planet, and communicating this can be really difficult at the start. The key is simplifying it down.

When I was first starting on my art journey, drawing people or characters was really difficult. I couldn't seem to make my drawings look how I wanted them too. They looked wobbly and boring and didn't resemble the other character work I had seen and admired. I would paw over other great artists whose work I admired like, Bernie Wrightson, Jim Lee and Frank Frazetta, and wonder how I could get my work up to their standard?

So, I did what a lot of beginner artists do, I tried to find a way around drawing, rather than actually tackling the problem of how to improve my drawings and technique. The reason for this I think is because of the complexity of the images and characters I was looking at and inspired by. If you look at any artist's work, it is natural as a beginner artist to try and jump straight to the level they are at. But the reality is you can't just pick up a pencil or stylus and create amazing works of art. It takes practice and determination. It was only when I really began to research how these artists worked that I discovered what it would take to get close to their level.

I found that my favourite artists when drawing and painting characters and compositions, worked on a large to small basis. They would build the big shapes first and only when they were happy with the composition would they move onto medium and small details. This was a massive turning point for me, seeing my heroes on Youtube videos spelling out the process. And now, this is the only way that I work. When constructing environments, I work with the biggest shapes first, mountains, castles, hills, sky, etc. For character, it's the same, start with the chest and hips and move smaller after these elements are correct.

STUDIES

Studies is a term used to describe using a photograph or existing works, to draw or paint from. This is the fastest way to improve your work and is something that all the great artists do on a regular basis. This process of doing studies is about taking an image that interests you and painting it to better understand elements contained within it.

For good ways to level up your character related work good studies to do are of existing artists work that you like. This would involve painting out the shape/silhouette of the character piece you are using. It's amazing how much information the silhouette communicates, and this exercise is a good one to use in order to understand it.

LIFE DRAWING

Life drawing is the process of drawing a living figure. Life drawing has been taught in colleges and universities for over a century and is one of the key exercises you should be doing as a character concept artist.

The figures you draw should show as much of the body as possible in order to capture the anatomy of the figure. Wherever possible you should be drawing from a live figure so you can capture the nuance of the person, in the same way that drawing outside in the environment is beneficial to environment concept art. However, the next best option is drawing from reference. This is where websites like Line of Action are great. https://line-of-action.com/

Websites like this mean you are able to generate a series of dynamic character poses and draw them in your home any time you like. This is a great way to practice with very low maintenance.

Task: Life drawing 20-minute sketches

Using the Line of Action website or any other that you would like to use and draw out 5–10 people.

- Try to relax and enjoy the process.
- Don't focus on detail, only the big shapes to start with.
- I tend to start with the chest, then move onto the hips, this tends to get me the best results.
- Keep your lines loose and expressive.
- Take about 20 minutes for each sketch.

Life drawing.

Drawing out the human body can be really difficult to get right but just focus on the big shapes and the flow of the body.

STUDIES OF PARTS OF THE BODY

I remember when at college, I really struggled with anatomy. I remember my tutor calling me out on this. All the characters I drew were hidden behind objects. This is because I couldn't draw legs. My tutor told me to just do studies of legs. So, I did, for a solid week that's all I drew, and it worked. The next assignment I did had a character free from things I would usually rely on to block my character's legs. But then my tutor pointed out the hands I drew, which were terrible. So, again I asked my tutor's advice. What can I do to improve this? He gave the same advice back to me again. "Just draw hands for a week". And it worked, I stopped asking after that. What he did gave me a very simple way of solving problems in my work. When I struggled with drawing or painting something, I spent time drawing/painting it until it worked. I advise all my students to do the same.

There are always going to be weaknesses in the work you produce. And that's ok. It's your job to highlight these and then work to fix them. The truth is that your work will always have areas that aren't as strong as some other areas. But it is important that we keep practicing and working hard on how to build on your process.

Another good way to improve your character design work is to draw real people in their natural environment. I used to do this a lot, and I built this in my daily life many years ago. I used to go to a local coffee shop, order a coffee, and that bit is important, you will get some funny looks and might even be evicted from the shop you are in, and draw the people around me. These sketches were relatively quick, 15–20-minute sketches. I found that there were some real benefits to doing this on a regular basis. The first was obviously the experience of drawing people, and all the technical things that go along with it. The second was the speed at which I had to work to capture the pose of the people I was drawing. The speed I had to work really focused me to think about what were the most important things in order to communicate the person I was drawing? Finally, drawing and observing people for this moment in time every day really helped how I would design people. All the people I were seeing had different combinations of age, gender, occupations and reasons for being in this place, at this time. And if these real people were interesting as characters in their own right, I could use some of these principles when designing my own characters.

Task: Drawing and painting bones

The next task we are going to do is sketching bones. Sketching bones is a really good exercise to do if you are wanting to improve your character drawing skills.

Bones are the framework that holds most creatures together. Drawing these will give you useful insights into how the body works. Bones are also unfamiliar organic shapes, meaning we don't see them that often in our everyday life. This means that our eyes and brains find it hard to pick up on any tiny mistakes when drawing them. I find this very useful when you are starting on your drawing journey.

- Choose five different types of bones from the reference link provided.
- Draw out the bones you have chosen.
- Start with the big shape first, then the medium and small shapes.
- Take 15–20 minutes per sketch.

https://uk.pinterest.com/lees0301/bones/

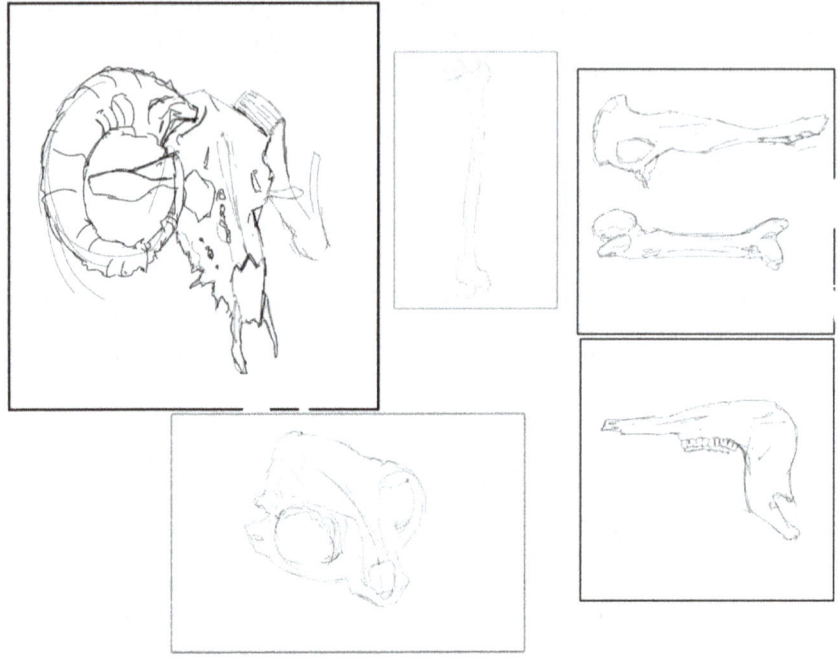

Bones.

These are loose sketches, so the only detail added is to help with the read of the object I am drawing.

STICK PEOPLE

I think we are all familiar with what a stick person is and looks like. At some point in our lives, we have all drawn a stick person. Stick drawings are simplified sketches of humans, typically. Drawing stick people is an important skill, and a skill that can be extremely useful in understanding character design. One of the inherent benefits with stick people drawing is the nature of the end product. The fact that the end product is lacking in overall detail is the point. We are just interested in the gesture and the framework that shows it, i.e., the sticks that make up the person. Drawing stick people is just about capturing the structure of the person of character as simply as possible.

When trying to skill up on human anatomy and character design in general, I used to spend a couple of hours a day drawing people in a natural environment. I used to grab a coffee with a sketchbook and try and capture some of the people around me. This was great because using stick people to capture their poses had to be quick and capture the main anatomical forms. Because the space I chose was a transient space, it necessitated me to use a technique that just focused on capturing the form and only focusing on simple forms. The key areas that you should be focusing on in terms of anatomy are the ball shapes for the ribs, hips and heads, and long lines for legs and arms.

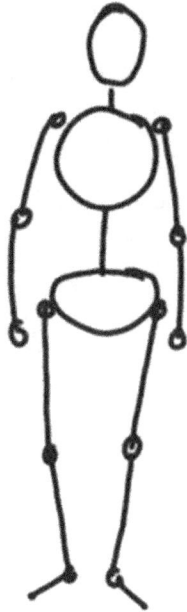

Stick figure.

Simplification is always the aim when communicating and in the case of humans, the centre masses can then be used to anchor the long bones.

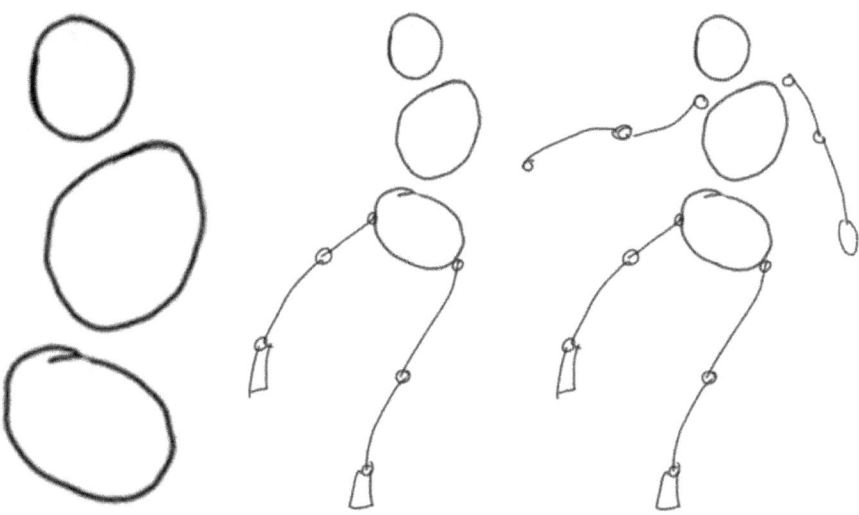

Centre masses. With legs. With arms and legs.

For me, however, one of the most important things that can be learned from this process of drawing stick people in a natural environment is how different everyone is. I'm not just talking about how different people are from an anatomical sense, like size and shape but also, from a design perspective. We are all creatures of our environment.

When coming up with characters for games and film, there is a lot of opportunity for variety. If you ask someone to build a sci-fi character, exploring the unknown reaches of the galaxy. There are so many options for clothing and accessories, nothing is off the table in terms of design. Ask someone to design a real-life person and this can be difficult. I think the main reason for this is because we see them every day. We are so familiar with everyday people we almost don't see their unique design. And drawing stick people in situ is a great way of unlocking this.

Task: Draw 50 stick people using photo reference

Using the Line of Action website or comparable website you are now going to draw 50 stick people. This is one of these exercises where you can work in a sketchbook if you want or digitally.

The aim when using reference to draw stick people is to try and capture the gesture and bone structure of the figure.

Start by grabbing ten or so pieces of figure reference. The reason for ten is so once you have the reference, you can concentrate on just drawing. With these first ten, you should be aiming to take no longer that 30 minutes. This is quite long for a series of stick people drawings, but it's important that you take your time and just concentrate on accurately representing the reference.

After the initial ten, you can just start grabbing a bunch of reference figures at a time and drawing as you see fit. Keep the same structure of body, pelvis, head and then moving to the long bones, but just try a little faster and more fluid.

- Grab at least 10 pieces of reference first before starting your drawings.
- Relax and don't worry about the process of drawing.
- Start with the centre masses of ribs and pelvis.
- Now add the long bones and head.
- Take no longer than 5 minutes per sketch.

Multiple stick figures.

These 4-minute sketches start with the ribs and hips, only when these are accurate, I will add the head and long bones.

Task: Draw 20 stick people out in the wild

So now that you are comfortable with drawing stick people from reference, I now would recommend doing what we talked about earlier in this section, drawing stick people while in a public space.

This can be quite daunting and a little weird at first, but don't worry, it will help with your character design work, and it will be fun.

The first thing is to sit down, relax and look around to see who might be good to turn into a stick person. Then draw them out and move onto the next one.

- Get set up in the space and choose someone to draw.
- Relax and don't worry about the process of drawing.
- Start with the centre masses of ribs and pelvis.
- Now add the long bones and head.
- Take no longer than 5 minutes per sketch.

Chapter 15

Sculptures and statues

SCULPTURES

Drawing and painting sculptures is a great place to sharpen your observational skills. By their nature, sculptures are abstract objects by design. These objects often stick out in the environment they occupy, often making their shape easy to distinguish, which is great for painting and drawing.

I have found that the process of drawing and painting sculptures acts as a really good link between the importance of understanding shape design and how you can leverage this in creating character concept art. Now this might seem like a bit of a leap. How can drawing and painting sculptures help with designing characters. The answer is how abstract objects inherently communicate to the viewer and how these objects make the viewer feel. We can use these principles when designing characters. You don't need to have a vast amount of detail on the things you create. Also, the abstractness of the things you create are a great way of injecting ambiguity in your work. Ambiguity in the initial stages of character design is a good thing; it gives the viewer an opportunity to imagine.

Justice sculpture. Abstract sculpture.

If we look at the images above of sculptures found around the city you live in or near, we can see how abstract shapes and compositions can tell stories and convey complex emotions.

DOI: 10.1201/9781003500032-15

Task: Drawing sculptures

For this task we are going to draw and paint sculptures from reference.

- Select three sculptures from the reference link provided.
- Sketch out the sculptures you have chosen.
- Take around 20–30 minutes for each sketch.

https://uk.pinterest.com/lees0301/sculptures/

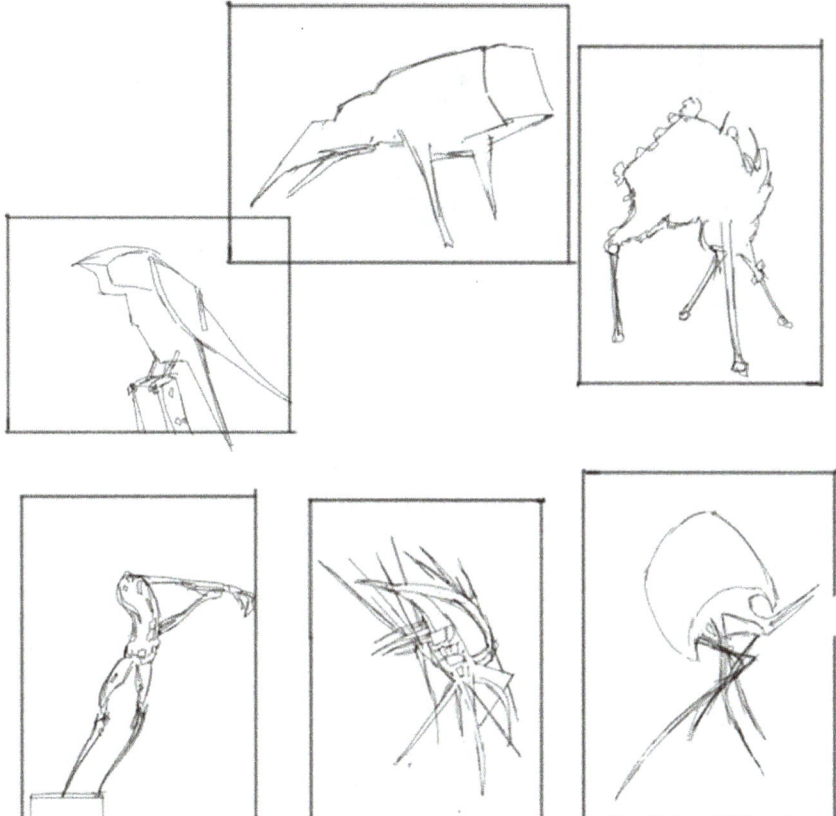

Sculpture drawings.

Using visual reference, I sketched out the outside shapes of the sculptures and then focused on elements that would communicate the shape of the sculpture.

Task: Painting sculptures

For this exercise, we will build upon the previous task and now use painting as our primary technique. As we have discussed before, drawing and painting are two quite different techniques, and this exercise is designed to explore this.

- Select another three sculptures from the reference link above.
- Paint out the sculptures you have chosen.
- Focus just on the shapes.
- Take around 15–30 minutes for each painting.

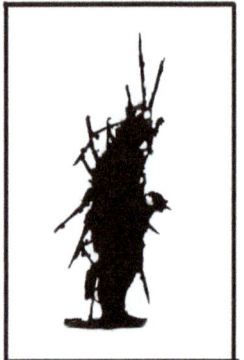  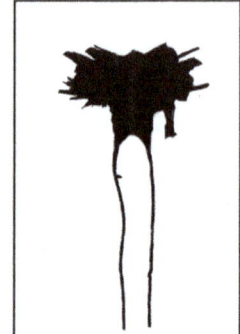

Three sculpture paintings.

STATUES

If you live in a town or city, the chances are you will have seen a statue at some point. Statues are often representations of real people, that aim to capture the essence of who they are or were and the things they contributed during their lifetime. They usually occupy an elevated site in the environment they live in. Like sculptures, this elevated silhouette makes it easy to make out their shape, and again, this makes them great for drawing and painting. Another added benefit in painting and drawing statues is because of their close relationship, in terms of likeness to the human figure. Moving from painting sculptures to statues is a nice transition for an artist and this also eases the transition when it comes to drawing and painting humans and characters, that we design.

Task: Drawing statues

This task is about drawing out statues in the same way we did with the sculptures task.

- Choose three statues from the reference link provided.
- Draw out the statues you have selected.

- Start with the big shapes first.
- Build detail off of the big shapes you draw.
- Take around 20–30 minutes for each sketch.

https://uk.pinterest.com/lees0301/statues-statues/

Task: Painting statues

- Choose another three statues from the reference link above.
- Paint out the statues you have selected.
- Start by painting out the big shapes you see.
- Only move onto the medium and small details once you are happy with the size and placement of the big shapes.
- Take 20 minutes for each painting.

https://uk.pinterest.com/lees0301/statues-statues/

Statues.

If you feel confident in capturing shapes in two simple values, white and black, then try adding a third value to add deeper levels of detail on the form itself.

Chapter 16

Character design

MANNEQUINS

A mannequin is a term referring to a character template used to design on. This character template is used to speed up your process as a concept artist. A mannequin would be used to get your designs down quicker.

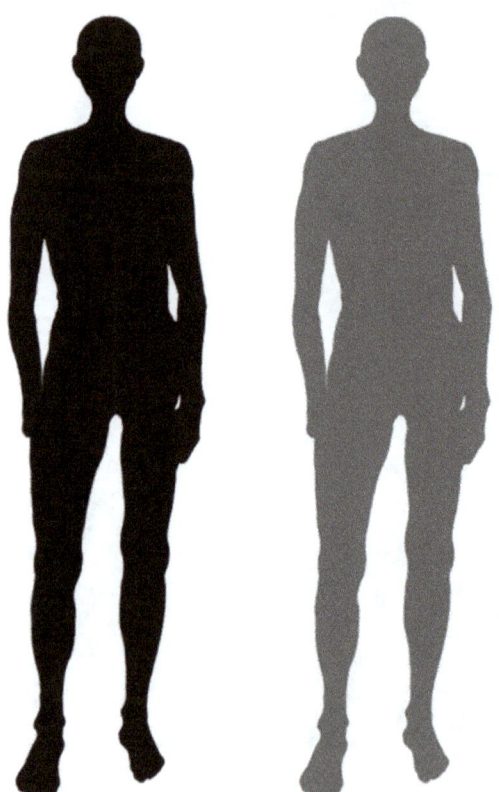

Black silhouette. Grey silhouette.

DOI: 10.1201/9781003500032-16

You can use dark or light mannequins to paint on, but external shape must be the primary aim when designing a character.

Sometimes, depending on the project you are working on, you may be given a character template to work from. This usually happens when the character you are designing is a standard male or female character archetype. However, if you are a designer starting out, you should be building your own character mannequins. There are a number of reasons for this that I cover below:

- Painting or drawing your own character templates/mannequins will make you focus on the anatomical importance of the characters you intend to design.
- It will help you appreciate how tight the silhouette and external character shape must be in order to design on top of it.
- It will focus you on thinking about the character without any detail or designs first.
- You will be able to use this again and again if the mannequin is correctly constructed.
- It will avoid any plagiarism issues with using an existing design or template.
- You may uncover some interesting things you hadn't thought of whilst building your mannequin.

Drawing and painting these character models/mannequins is an important part of the character design process for beginner artists.

Understanding the shape and form of the character you intend to design is the first step we need to learn in order to free up your design process.

Once the character mannequin is completed, you can then use this to paint on top of. Before I start the painting and working through the design process, I drag out a copy of the mannequin. This is so I can keep a copy of the original design and go back to this if necessary. One of the main reasons I would go back to this is if I want a hard reset on my designs, after I have iterated. It's easy to go down a few rabbit holes with designs, and having a clear starting mannequin is often invaluable.

STEP BY STEP MANNEQUIN

When creating character designs, it's important that you have a place to house your design ideas. One way of doing this is by designing a mannequin. A mannequin is a semi-generic character model, that you can effectively dress, with your design ideas on.

Designing a character mannequin is a really important starting point in the character design process. Obviously, we need to have some rough idea what type of character this is before we paint out our mannequin. Otherwise, you might paint out a character that is way too different from the archetype you are aiming at.

Simple statement.

The aim at the start of painting is to get the rough masses of the figure in the right spots, this is known as the simple statement or first read. This is the most important part of the painting stage.

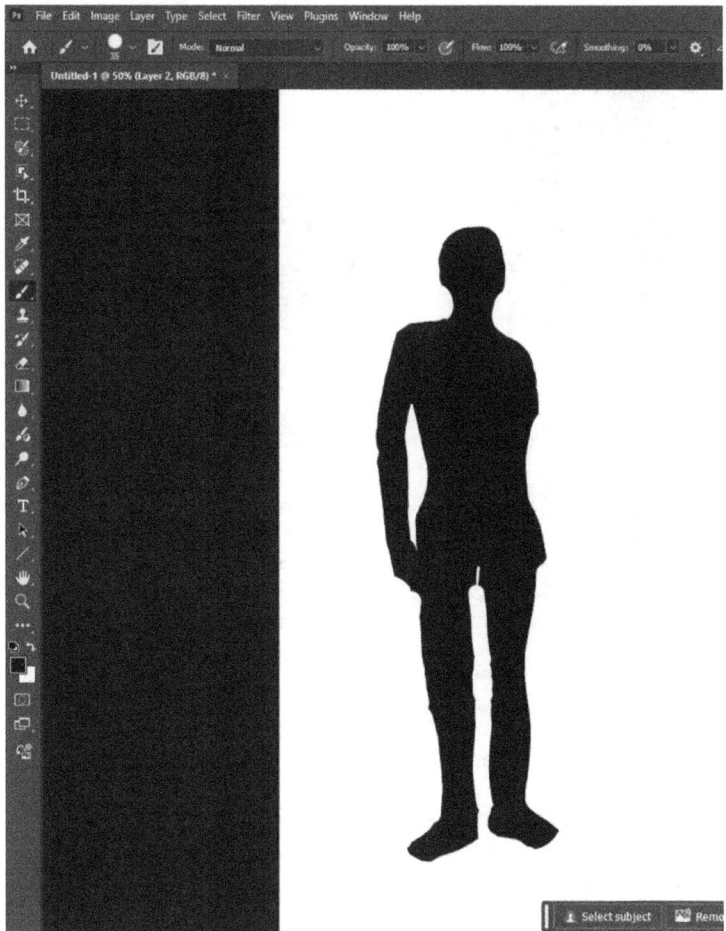

Refined simple statement.

From this you then carve the rough proportions out of the initial shapes. Continuously look back and forth in between the painting and the reference you are using.

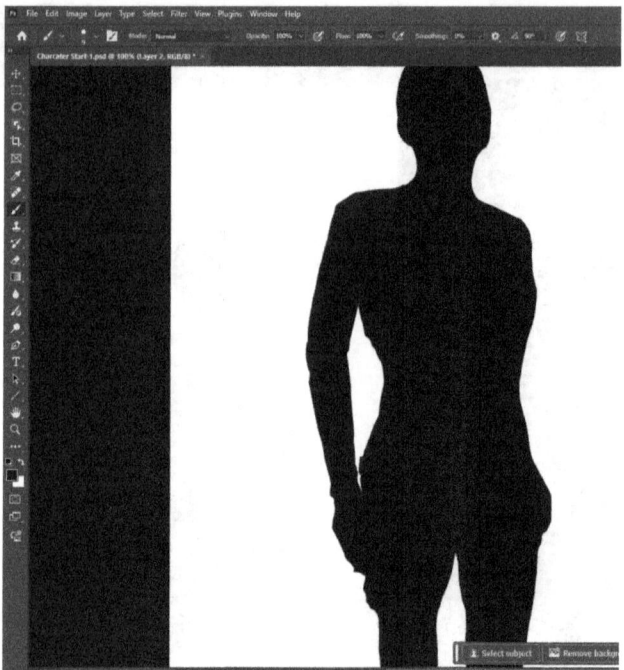

More refinement.

Once you have the rough shape, start to refine edges and tighten up the mannequin.

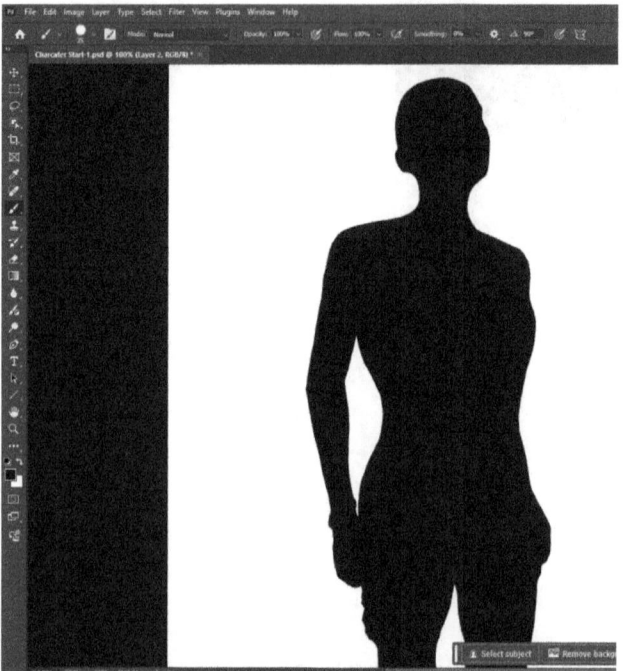

Smoother.

Really focus on getting the silhouette as accurate as possible and continue to work your way around the figure.

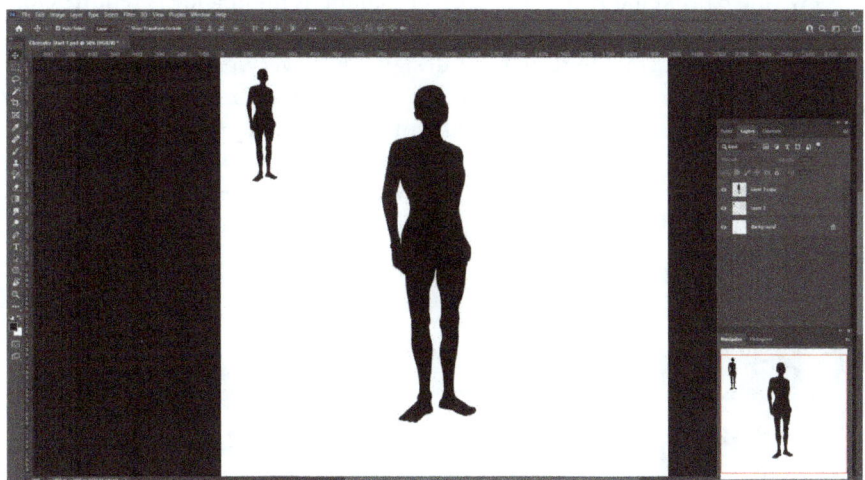

Saving the first version.

The mannequin is now complete. We can now use this to design on but make sure you create a copy of the base one to work on each time. Just in case you need to start from this position again.

Below is a link to a body visualiser website, where you are able to change the parameters of the human body and show their effects. You are also able to rotate the figure, which can be really helpful to draw from and use as reference. This might be a useful tool to look at if drawing and painting reference isn't working for you.

https://bodyvisualizer.is.tue.mpg.de/male.html

Task: Paint out a mannequin

For this task, you are going to paint out a mannequin that we will then use to paint our ideas onto.

- Find real reference to use as a guide.
- Make sure the reference you are using has tight fitting clothing, so you can see the anatomy.
- Start with the big shapes first.
- Take as long as you need to paint out the refined mannequin.

Once you have a semi-generic character mannequin painted out (like above), it is now time to paint your designs on top of the mannequin. However, before we do this, we are going to need ideas to work with. This as we have discussed before is a designer's main currency.

As we have broken down in the previous chapter, finding ideas requires lots of visual references and research. Once we have appropriate amount of visual references, we can start iterating out designs. For every page of around 8–10 images that I have on a moodboard, I will get around 2–3 designs. It's also important to have a tonal moodboard handy when designing your characters to make sure they feel like tonally they belong to the world you are designing for. These tonal moodboards we have covered in the research section of this book, but just as they sound they represent the tone and feel of the world you are designing for.

Armour moodboard.

I sometimes find it useful to have some core character traits written down when I'm designing, to ground the character and keep me on track when producing designs. These can be anything that drives the character and motivates them. I often start with five character traits to hold the design together. These traits should be a part of the character you are designing. So, things like...

- Do they have children?
- What are their fears?
- Who do these characters have relationships with?

- Who do they respect?
- What traumatic events have they encountered?
- What motivates them and why?

All of these things and others like it are good ways to start the design process.

Mannequin.

ITERATING CHARACTER MODELS

With your mannequin now painted out to a good level, a bunch of visual reference to inspire you, and 5-character traits to guide you. It's now time to design our characters. The first step is to paint out some of the ideas onto your first mannequin. Before you do this though save a undesigned mannequin, so you can go back to this starting point if your designs get too wild or go off in the wrong direction. I call this the zero design. Start with your most obvious ideas first and paint directly on the silhouette of the mannequin. We are just using the same colour as the existing mannequin and pulling out forms and painting in cloths and how they would look as a plain silhouette. This is really important and will really help you appreciate how important the shape of the character is. It's incredible how much detail you can get just with one simple value on a white background. If you force yourself to work like this, with limitations, psychologically, it will really help.

DESIGNING A CHARACTER

Now we are on to the fun part, the designing of the character. The best way to approach this is by just exploring ideas and shapes on your character mannequin. How you should approach this is by heavily relying on reference when starting out. When grabbing reference to use for character ideas, try to use parts of the reference and don't just reproduce ideas wholly that already exist.

ENVIRONMENT MOODBOARD FOR CHARACTER

When designing characters, your instinct might be to dive straight in and start grabbing reference, hats, coats, amazing props. However, an alternative to this and the way I choose to work is by grabbing an environment reference moodboard. The reason for this is to establish what the world is that the character lives in. We are all symptomatic of the environments we inhabit, so having an environment moodboard as an anchor point for the characters I create is essential for keeping my designs on track. This moodboard shouldn't be extensive, so I try to keep it to one page.

Ruin moodboard.

This would be representative of a typical moodboard I would produce if I was aiming to design a medieval dark ages type of character.

I tend to grab say three pieces of reference spread across the body of the character for each iteration. So, one character silhouette might have reference for an interesting coat, boots and an item they are carrying. The next might have an interesting hairstyle, gloves and boots. The important thing is you keep varying your reference and think about these characters as real people within the world.

Work big and try to paint the big elements on your character designs first. These will then act as an anchor point for the medium and small parts.

Use the reference you have gathered for ideas and as a guide to the shapes you should be drawing on your character mannequin. It is really easy, for instance, when painting out a hat or something to paint what you think a hat looks like, rather than the actual shape that the hat you have as reference has. This is one of the major reasons that works you create look off. Our brain loves to simplify and as artists starting out, we often fall into the trap of drawing the object rather than the shape it is in the reference.

Character silhouette iteration.

At this stage, just focus on getting the essence of the character you are trying to create. For each silhouette you are iterating, you should take around 15–30 minutes. This should give you long enough to get your big ideas for the character blocked out.

Task: Create a series of character designs

For this task, you are going to use the mannequin you have just painted to design on. Grab reference to guide you and start with a character type in mind.

- Grab reference to guide you, three or four for each character design.
- Just focus on the shape detail to explain who the character is.

- Start with the big shapes first.
- Once you are happy with one, then move onto the next.
- Try and do as many designs as you can.
- Take around 15–20 minutes per idea.

Final chose silhouette.

Conclusion

Well done for getting this far and I hope the information and tasks within this book have set you on your way to being creative. I hope it's clear just how important the fundamentals are when it comes to creating strong environment and character concepts. Things like drawing, painting, composition and especially silhouette and shape design are not just technical exercises, they're the core of how we communicate visually.

The importance of shape design and the silhouette of an object or character is the first impression a viewer gets, and often, it tells more of the story than a detailed rendering could ever do. That's why starting with strong shapes and simple values is so important. Not showing everything gives the viewer space to imagine and this is why these techniques are such a powerful tool.

Drawing and painting are your tools for exploration and expression. They help you think, experiment and solve creative problems. Whether you're building vast landscapes or shaping the personality of a character, your ability to design with emotion is what brings the idea to life.

So, keep practicing, observing and creating.

Thank you.

> Inspiration is for amateurs. The rest of us just show up and get to work. If you wait around for the clouds to part and a bolt of lightning to strike you in the brain, you are not going to make an awful lot of work. All the best ideas come out of the process; they come out of the work itself.
>
> Chuck Close

DOI: 10.1201/9781003500032-17

Bibliography

3DTotal Publishing. (2022). *Anatomy for Artists: Drawing Form and Pose.*

3DTotal Publishing. (2020). *Art Fundamentals: Color, Light, Composition, Anatomy, Perspective and Depth.*

3DTotal Publishing. (2019). *Beginner's Guide to Sketching: Robots, Vehicles and Sci-fi Concepts.*

3DTotal Publishing. (2016). *Beginner's Guide to Digital Painting in Photoshop: Sci-Fi and Fantasy.*

3DTotal Publishing. (2022). *Beyond Art Fundamentals: A Guide to Emotion, Mood, Storytelling for Artists.*

3DTotal Publishing. (2018). *Digital Painting in Photoshop: Industry Techniques for Beginners.*

3DTotal Publishing. (2016). *Master the Art of Speed Painting: Digital Painting Techniques.*

Bacher, H. (2008). *Dream Worlds: Production Design for Animation.* Focal Press.

Bacher, H. (2015). *Sketchbook: Composition Studies for Film.* Laurence King.

Bacher, H., & Suryavanshi, S. (2018). *Vishon: Colour and Composition for Film.* Laurence King.

Bang, M. (2000). *Picture This: How Pictures Work.* Chronicle Books.

Bridgman, G. B. (1971). *Bridgman's Complete Guide to Drawing From Life.* Sterling.

Clare, J., Fowkes, N., Kurtz, D. E., Lay, D., & Rutkowski, G. (2023). *Artist Masters Series: Composition and Narrative.* 3DTotal Publishing.

Fowkes, N. (2016). *How to Draw Portraits in Charcoal.*

Frederick, M. (2007). *101 Things I Learned in Architecture School.* MIT Press.

Hillkurtz, A. (2021). *Sketching Techniques for Artists.*

Holmes, M. T. (2014). *The Urban Sketcher.* North Light Books.

Jones, A. (2015). *Heaven's Hell: The Art of Anthony Jones.*

Jones, W. (2011). *Making Marks: Architects' Sketchbooks – The Creative Process.* Thames & Hudson.

LaCoste, R. (2021). *Worlds: The Art of Raphael LaCoste.* Caurette.

Lilly, E. (2015). *The Big Bad World of Concept Art for Video Games: An Insider's Guide for Students.* Design Studio Press.

Lilly, E. (2017). *The Big Bad World of Concept Art for Video Games: How to Start Your Career as a Concept Artist.* Design Studio Press.

Loomis, A. (1947). *Creative Illustration.* Viking Press.

Mateu-Mestre, M. (2010). *Framed Ink: Drawing and Composition for Visual Storytellers.* Design Studio Press.

Mateu-Mestre, M. (2019). *Framed Ink Volume 2: Frame, Format, Energy, and Composition for Visual Storytellers.* Design Studio Press.

Mateu-Mestre, M. (2016). *Framed Perspective Vol. 1.* Design Studio Press.

Mateu-Mestre, M. (2019). *Framed Drawing Techniques*. Design Studio Press.
Mateu-Mestre, M. (2022). *Framed Environment Design*. Design Studio Press.
Muftic, K. (2017). *Figure Drawing for Concept Artists*. 3DTotal Publishing.
Payne, E. A. (2005). *Composition of Outdoor Painting* (7th ed.). DeRu's Fine Arts.
Robertson, S. (2013). *How to Draw: Drawing and Sketching Objects and Environments from Your Imagination*. Design Studio Press.
Ruppel, R. (2014). *Graphic L.A.* Design Studio Press.
Schellewald, C. (2006). *LASF: A Sketchbook from California*.
Sparth. (2015). *Structura 3: The Art of Sparth*.
Speed, H. (1913). *The Practice and Science of Drawing*. Dover Publications.
Stanchfield, W. (2009). *Drawn to Life: The Walt Stanchfield Lectures, Volume One*. Focal Press.
Stanchfield, W. (2009). *Drawn to Life: The Walt Stanchfield Lectures, Volume Two*. Focal Press.
Tyler, P. (2017). *Drawing and Painting the Landscape*. Crowood Press.
Agerer, M. S. (2020). *Start Drawing Landscapes: Basic Principles, Composition, and Exercises*.

Useful links

MY PAGES

My Pinterest Page: https://www.pinterest.co.uk/lees0301/
My Artstation Page: https://www.artstation.com/stocks/following

VIDEOS ENVIRONMENT CONCEPT ART

Victor Staris: https://www.youtube.com/channel/UCkMK-WJFcixvnKVJcx_9DQQ/videos
Jordan Grimmer: https://www.youtube.com/@JordanGrimmer
Jose Vega: https://www.youtube.com/@ArtofJoseVega
Grady Frederick: https://www.youtube.com/@gradyfrederickart
Tim McBurnie: https://www.youtube.com/@TheDrawingCodex
FZD Design School: https://www.youtube.com/@FZDSCHOOL

CHARACTER CONCEPT ART

Robot Pencil: https://www.youtube.com/@Robotpencildesign
Hardy Fowler: https://www.youtube.com/@fowlerillus
Proko: https://www.youtube.com/@ProkoTV

GENERAL CONCEPT ART AND PAINTING

Trent Kaniuga: https://www.youtube.com/@TrentKaniuga
BRD: https://www.youtube.com/@BillyRobertsDesignz
Learn Squared: https://www.youtube.com/@learnsquared
Janos Gerasch: https://www.youtube.com/@Janos.Artzone
Billy Roberts: https://www.youtube.com/@BillyRobertsDesignz

Marco Bucci: https://www.youtube.com/@marcobucci
Ian Roberts: https://www.youtube.com/@IanRobertsMasteringComposition

LIFE DRAWING WEBSITE

https://line-of-action.com/practice-tools

Index

For Product Safety Concerns and Information please contact our EU
representative GPSR@taylorandfrancis.com
Taylor & Francis Verlag GmbH, Kaufingerstraße 24, 80331 München, Germany

www.ingramcontent.com/pod-product-compliance
Lightning Source LLC
Chambersburg PA
CBHW060852170526
45158CB00001B/327

* 9 7 8 1 0 3 2 7 6 9 8 9 9 *